THE

SUICIDE

GIFT

THE SUICIDE GIFT

Steven Fredrick Macek, Esq.

STELIX PUBLISHING

STELIX PUBLICATION

700 Pleasant Street

Suite LL05

New Bedford, MA 02740

©2023 by Steven Fredrick Macek

Book design and layout:

ISBN: 979-8-9893983-0-0 (hardcover)

ISBN: 979-8-9893983-1-7 (paperback)

Library of Congress Cataloguing-in-Publication Data

Macek, Steven Fredrick

The Suicide Gift

Psychic ability I. Title

BF1031.E44 2023

133.8-dc22

2010021141

Printed in the United States of America

www.stelixpublishing.com

DEDICATON

This book is dedicated to my husband, Elix Cintron (aka *Coach Elix*). The universe granted me the greatest gift on April 8, 1993, the day I met you. You have the most compassionate soul of anybody I have ever met. You have taught me to always strive to be the best version of myself and you are always there to assist me in any way you can.

If I need to be reincarnated due to a lesson I need to learn, it would never be to fall in love. My soul has checked that off its list. You can't beat perfection. I love you forever Elix.

ACKNOWLEDGEMENTS

Thank you, Claire, my mom. You stayed by my side my entire life and you were my biggest cheerleader. Your goal in life was to take care of your two boys, and you mastered that goal. If I were to come back to earth repeatedly, I would only do it if you were my mom each time. I love you pussycat. Thank you, William, my dad. It took me a long time to figure out that you loved me enough to leave me so I could realize my passion and purpose in life. You have always been my shining star. Thank you Fredrick, Anna, and Stefan, my grandparents. I never knew you in the physical world but your energy around me can't be denied. Thank you, Rose, my remaining grandparent, and my ride or die. You also crossed over before I was born but I know you are always with me. It must be possible to feel unconditional love from someone you never physically met because you give that to me every day. I can't wait to see you when I walk through the white light, I know you will be front and center. Thank you Snowy, Dante, Rico, Little Ricky, Memphis, a.k.a. Monkey, Jango, and all the other pets that have been part of our family.

TABLE OF
CONTENTS

INTRODUCTION

+ ◆ +

January 19, 2023

I am sitting in the bridal suite at The Barn at Wight Farm in Sturbridge, Massachusetts, waiting for a text to tell me they are ready for me. I receive the text and head out the door of the suite. I cross a small driveway to get to the building the event is in, and it is raining mixed with sleet. I enter the building and peek into the large room to see approximately 125 people sitting at tables, waiting for me. The director introduces me, and I walk into the room. It's showtime.

CHAPTER 01

THE EIGHT-YEAR-OLD BOY

It was August 25 and it was very warm. A typical summer day in Providence, Rhode Island where I grew up. I was eight years old, and I remember being in my bedroom sitting on my bed and reading a comic book. I started noticing loud voices coming from the kitchen but didn't think too much about it. We lived in a three-decker house that my parents owned. We, my parents and my older brother, lived on the first floor and there were tenants that rented the 2nd and 3rd floors.

Moments after hearing the loud voices, my mother came rushing into my bedroom, grabbed my arm, and said come with me while she was pulling me towards the bedroom door. I had no idea what was going on. The tenant, Patsy, who lived on the third floor with her husband and nine-year-old daughter, was standing in the kitchen. Patsy and my mom were very good friends. Patsy grabbed my hand and forcibly pulled me through the hallway and outside. She brought me to the neighbor's yard where she stayed with me. I remember I continuously asked Patsy what was going on and she just kept repeating, "Everything is okay."

It's November, three months later, and I can hear my Aunt Dolores saying to my mom, "I don't understand why you need to go back, I think you should stay longer." I walked into one of the bedrooms at my aunt's house and my mom had a suitcase on the bed and was placing our clothes in the suitcase. She looked at me and said, "We are going home today."

The last thing I remember, I was standing with Patsy in my neighbor's yard in August. It's now November and apparently we have been living with my aunt and her husband, Uncle Jackie, for the last three months. I have no recollection of the past three months. What happened to my memory? How can three months disappear from my mind? Did something happen to me that I don't remember? Maybe something is mentally wrong with me. I couldn't understand this, but my memory picks up the day we are leaving my aunt's house to go back home.

My mom Claire had three sisters whom she was extremely close to and loved very much. On the way to our house, all three sisters were part of the procession in their respective cars. Patsy, her husband, and her daughter were all on the back steps waving and welcoming us home. The second-floor tenants were also there with big smiles on their faces. Once Patsy saw my mother step out of the car she started crying. My mother followed suit very quickly and before I knew it, mostly everyone was crying to some degree.

We walked into the house, and it smelled very musty but warm. From what my mother told me, I cried entering the house and was attached to her side the entire time. My brother walked independently throughout the house. My aunts all said they wanted to stay with us for a couple of days, but my mom told them the three of us were okay and she would prefer for us to be by ourselves. That night, when it was time for bed, all three of us went into my mother's bedroom and slept in her full-size bed. Both my brother and I were afraid to sleep alone in our bedrooms so the three of us slept in her bed together for a while. That first night, as I was about to go to sleep, I realized something was different. I didn't feel the same but couldn't figure out if it was the house or if it had something to do with me.

I am not sure when I realized my dad was no longer there. I do remember at some point my mom telling me and my brother that we were going to tell people that he died of a heart attack. For years I had that script in my head and repeated it to anyone who asked what happened to my dad.

My dad had a workshop in our basement, so he spent a lot of time down there. On August 25, my mom went down to the basement to tell him dinner was ready. She found him hanging from the rafters and at that point, he was dead. My dad went down to the basement earlier that afternoon, and took his life.

My dad was in the Navy for over twenty years and when he retired, he never felt the same sense of satisfaction or appreciation as he did in the Navy. He was a big drinker but that increased after he retired from the Navy. A very big crate fell off a shelf in one of the jobs my dad had, and it hit him on the head. My mom always said he was never the same after that accident. I believe my dad got very depressed and the increase in alcohol consumption made the situation even worse. There were times at three in the morning my dad would get out of bed, open the kitchen door, and go outside with no shoes or shirt on. He would make comments that would not make sense and my mother would have to convince him to come back into the house.

My dad on his wedding day, 1954

I know how much my parents loved each other. When I was selling the house we grew up in, I found a shoebox buried in a deep chest. I had never seen this before and when I opened up the box, I realized it was a stack of letters my dad wrote to my mom when he was in the Navy. A couple of days later, on a Sunday, I woke up early, made coffee, and sat on the living room couch with the box. I opened every letter, approximately fifty of them, and read every word. They included things like, "I miss you so much," "In ninety days I will see you and I'm counting the days," and "I love you so much honey." The emotions were overwhelming as I held the letters and read the contents.

I also knew how much my dad loved his two boys. We were everything to him. It has taken many years of therapy to stop blaming myself and feeling like my dad took his life because I wasn't good enough. I'm not sure if I knew I was gay at eight years old, but I knew I was different. I'm not completely healed but I have hope I will be at some point. One thing is for sure, I have made significant progress since this tragedy and will continue with this progression for as long as I need.

The following summer, when it started getting hot, my mom would leave her bed in the middle of the night when we were sleeping. She would try to move quietly and would go into my bedroom to sleep. It wasn't long before I realized she was not in bed so I would follow her into my bedroom and got into my bed with her to sleep. At some point, my mom would get up again and leave my bedroom with me in the bed and go to my brother's bedroom. That lasted for a couple of years and eventually, my mom told my brother he needed to start sleeping in his own bedroom and finally all three of us were in our respective bedrooms.

I don't have many memories of my dad but the ones I have make me smile. As an eight-year-old boy when my father died, I should have many more memories of him but so much of my memory was erased after he died.

On my dad's side of the family, he had four siblings, and they had a big presence with us after he died. After a while, the visits were happening less. My mom was so close to her sisters, we were always with them.

My mom used to tell me that she could feel my dad in the house, and she knew that he was always around the three of us and watching over us. That always made me feel so comforted, but why couldn't I feel my dad around me? I felt sad when I thought of him because it reminded me that he was no longer physically here with me. We would go to the cemetery periodically to visit my dad's and grandparents' gravestones and I never liked going there. I used to tell my mom I didn't want to go, and my brother and my mom could never understand that. They felt as if we were going to visit Dad and I couldn't explain it, but I felt almost worse after I went. I always had an empty feeling going to the cemetery, almost like staring at a rock for twenty minutes and then going home. On some level, I must have known my dad was with me all the time which would explain why the trip to the cemetery was not special to me.

One thing I remember, any place my mom was, I was. Being the youngest, my mom overcompensated and did everything for me, and I am sure part of the closeness to her was to ensure my remaining parent wasn't going to go anywhere without me.

As an adult, I've come to realize that I have had two very separate lives. The pre-eight-year-old boy and the post-eight-year-old boy. From being born to eight years old, I was a normal child, very happy and just being a little boy. I always felt very loved and never felt alone. One of the few memories I remember with my dad was him calling me "Pumpkin." He would lie on the couch and open his legs like a drawbridge opening and say, "Pumpkin, get in before the drawbridge closes." I would run and jump on the couch to be next to him.

My First Holy Communion

I also remember him taking us into the woods to pick mushrooms. He was a cook in the Navy for over twenty years and was great in the kitchen. All the mushrooms we picked were used in the dinner he made later that day. He also loved to fish. I have memories of him leaving in the middle of the night to go fishing and the ironic part was nobody ate fish except him.

His parents were from Poland and they could barely speak any English. He was one of five children and the baby. However, there were thirteen years between him and the next oldest sibling, so he was also very spoiled as a child. My mother was always quick to remind me that he thought he was the prince in his family, and deserved to always be treated like a prince.

My mother would take me and my brother to church on Sundays and he would stay at home and cook dinner. I loved when he made **golabki** or **pierogi**, traditional Polish food and he would talk to me in Polish. In third grade, the Polish Catholic school my brother and I were attending started offering Polish lessons on Saturdays. My brother wasn't interested but I jumped at the chance to learn more Polish. Not long after starting the classes, my dad died so I stopped attending those classes.

The post-eight-year-old boy changed dramatically. He became shy, filled with anxiety, decreased self-confidence, and concerned about what everybody else thought of him. He felt that he was not good enough.

Shame became his best friend but he realized right then that he would hide his best friend from everyone, no matter what he had to do.

My dad's siblings all lived near us except for his oldest brother who lived in Massachusetts. I liked it when they would come to visit because they were so different from my mom's side of the family. They would make me feel special and they were attentive. My mom and her sisters would fight one minute and be over it the next minute. It was much calmer when my dad's side came over. I do wish I maintained more of a relationship with my dad's side but more recently, with social media, I have gotten in contact with some cousins which has been a wonderful experience.

MY MATERNAL COUSIN HOLLY has always been a big part of my life. Two of my mom's sisters never had children and the other one only had one daughter. Her name is Holly and even though we are cousins, we're really more like brother and sister. We grew up together and became very close. At one point, Holly's parents owned a three-story house; they lived on the second floor and my two other aunts lived on the first floor and third floor. Their house was about a ten-minute drive. One winter we had a very big snowstorm, so Holly and I decided to leave our houses at the same time and walk toward each other. The halfway mark was a supermarket and that is where we met and went to buy something to eat. I loved the adventure,getting to see Holly, and spending time with her before we had to head back to our respective homes.

Holly's parents had a camper van, which came in handy when the entire family would go someplace. We could all jump into the van, and all be together in this one vehicle. On one family trip we went to a restaurant and before everyone was done eating, Holly and I said we were going to take a walk. We walked the grounds of the restaurant and found a big pen with chickens in it. We assumed those chickens would be the ones the restaurant would cook so we needed to save them. It took a lot of effort, but we managed to get the door open and told the chickens to run free. On the way out of the parking lot of the restaurant, my aunt yelled out, "Oh my god, look, there are chickens running everywhere!"

Another time, Holly and I decided to do something nice for our moms for Mother's Day and planned to cook breakfast for them. Then we invited our other two aunts and ultimately the entire extended family came to this breakfast. Everyone was instructed to stay in the living room and Holly and I would be in the kitchen doing the preparation and cooking breakfast.

We made pancakes and some other side dishes for breakfast. I remember mixing the batter for the pancakes but as I was mixing it, I noticed these black dots in the batter. I called Holly over and said what are these black dots? We couldn't figure it out at first but then realized the box of pancake batter had been sitting in the cabinet for, let's say, a **very** long time. The little black dots were bugs.

At that point, we had a choice: throw the batter away and not have pancakes (which were the highlight of the breakfast) or go forward making them and serve the bug pancakes. We decided to go forward and make them. Everyone loved the pancakes, and we got a lot of compliments on them. After breakfast was done and we cleaned up, Holly and I went to a restaurant for breakfast; we weren't going to eat those pancakes! Holly and I bring that story up periodically and sharing that story with my beautiful niece, Holly's daughter Morgan, is priceless!

One difference between the two boys living inside me was the pre-eight- year-old didn't have anxiety, or at least not in my memory. The post- eight-year-old had enormous amounts of anxiety. Anxiety that spun out of control for many years.

In grammar school, towards the seventh and eighth grades, I noticed other boys begin to bully me. I am sure they started noticing me being different, not being as masculine or into sports, and that difference generated bullying. Of course, that bullying added to my anxiety, and in some ways it also made me want to stay a child as long as I could.

My mom never remarried and always said her devotion was to her two boys, not to a man. My mom, Claire, passed away on February 12, 2020, three weeks short of her ninetieth birthday and right before the pandemic took over the world. She was the best mom anyone could ever have, and I miss her every day. I stayed with her the night before she crossed over and I just talked to her. My mom hadn't spoken in the last year before she died but that last night, holding her hand I said, "I love you," and she looked back at me and clearly responded with "I love you too." That night I felt like I could finally let go and she died the next morning. If she died one month later, I would have never had that opportunity to be with her due to Covid-19 and the visiting restrictions. I know that is why she selected that date to cross over. Right until the end, she was still taking care of me.

INSIGHT

My definition of spirit is any person, animal, plant, etc., that has lived on this earth and has died and transitioned back home, into the white light.

Trauma and specific events can create a roadblock on the path you are supposed to follow. Every individual has their own lane to drive in and many things can force us to take an exit off our paths, which steers us away from understanding our purpose, gifts, and goals. My dad taking his life when I was eight years old was a traumatic event in my life. That event changed my energy, my soul, and my universe without me being aware of the change. It rewired my internal hard drive which is so difficult to change back. That event prevented me from knowing I was a Medium, that I could communicate with the dead. The trauma created a blind spot for me that lasted decades. The first step to take to connect with spirit is to take an inventory of your life. Write down significant events that occurred in your life. Is there something you are holding on to? Is there something you don't want to address? Things in your past that have not been resolved create barriers between this world and the spirit world. I had no idea I was a Medium solely because I hadn't dealt with this tragedy in my life.

CHAPTER 2

ACTING OUT

I will never understand how, but my mom sent my brother and me to private schools right through twelfth grade. There were no discussions about school; she wanted the best education for both of us.

Growing up I had a vivid imagination. I would spend hours in my room playing with toy figurines and feeling like they were my friends and they were real. I loved puppets and putting on puppet shows. I still have the original Jim Henson puppets my mom bought for me years ago. What I didn't realize then, the connection was not with the figurines or puppets, it was with spirit.

My beloved Jim Henson puppets

I was an excellent student in grammar school, however as eighth grade approached, the clown in me became more evident. My grades always remained in the A category, but my conduct started becoming out of control. I went to a private, Catholic high school and it was a boy-only school. I was not thrilled because most of my friends were girls. In hindsight, I think my misbehavior in high school was a diversion from the sadness I was experiencing. I loved making my close friends laugh and would do almost anything to entertain them.

There was a family across the street from us and the parents had six kids. I became very friendly with two of the kids who were the closest to my age. The three of us were very mischievous, but somehow never got caught doing things we shouldn't have been doing. One day the three of us took the bus downtown to Providence and went into the Outlet Building, which was a department store. On the fifth floor, WJAR Channel 10 (local news station) had its studios there. I found a secret door that was unlocked and realized it was a way to get into the studios. We loved going there around 10 a.m. because there was always a baking segment on the 12 p.m. news and whatever the selection was for the day, we sampled them.

We once went into the studio and the weather map was prepared on this giant slab by using magic markers to fill in the country's weather. I erased the entire map and put a little wavy line on the top right corner of the map,then we ran out of the studio. I am sure the weatherman scrambled when he entered the studio, saw a blank slate and had to quickly recreate the map. I was so thrilled when we went to the TV section in the Outlet, waited for the weather segment on the news and I saw my wavy line, right there on the map on TV!

My best friend David and I in the television studio

I still have a picture of my best friend and me standing in front of that same weather map. Ironically, a couple of years ago I went to the new WJAR Channel 10 news studio (this time invited) and I shared that story with Frank Colletta, an anchorman, who remembers being in the old studio before they moved. He got a good laugh out of my story.

Freshman year of high school, my friends and I loved playing make-believe. At one point, we pretended to be **Charlie's Angels**, with me being Farrah Fawcett's character, Jill Munroe, of course. We also pretended we were bionic, like the **Six Million Dollar Man** and the **Bionic Woman**. We would move in slow motion and even try to make similar noises that the TV show would play when the characters were using their bionic features.

We were not typical children. One day hanging out one of us mentioned, "Wouldn't it be cool to get on the roof of the Howard Building downtown?" The Howard Building was in downtown Providence, and we would walk by it all the time. My mom, at some point, worked in that building. Well, that was all we needed to hear, and the goal now was to get to the tops of buildings anyway we could. More on that later.

In my senior year in high school, I decided to experiment with lightening my hair so I purchased a product that would give me highlights. The instructions said to wet your hair, spray Sun In in your hair and then go sit in the sun. The effect would be a lighter shade than your existing shade. My friend and I followed the instructions and after sitting in the sun for about one hour, our medium-dark brown hair now had a lot of orange highlights. We were aiming for blond, but that didn't quite happen.

The next couple of months I did some more experimenting with color, and I think I had every color that existed. Finally, I got bored and decided to let it grow out. I needed one more haircut to finally get rid of the remaining unnatural color in my hair and I would be back to where I started.

My neighbor was a stylist and she used to cut my hair in her house. She canceled about two or three scheduled appointments to cut my hair, so I asked my friend's sister, who was home from college, if she knew how to cut hair. It was not the brightest thing I ever asked but she responded with a yes. Both parents were working so I wet my hair and she started cutting. It looked fine while it was wet but when it dried, it looked like she cut my hair with a lawn mower. I managed to not let my mom notice my hair when I got home and the next day I called my neighbor, the stylist, and begged her to let me go to her house now because I had a disaster on top of my head. She said yes and I ran over to her house. I took my baseball cap off and her eyes opened wide and she yelled, "What the hell happened to your hair?" I told her what happened, and she immediately said, "Go wash your hair and I will try my best to fix this mess."

When she finished cutting my hair, I had a crew cut. My hair was the shortest I have ever had it. I was stunned. I have always had my hair moderately long, and I have always had very thick hair. It was like my mane of hair was no more. I knew my mother was going to have a fit when she saw my haircut.

Later on that day, I walked into my house and my mother looked at me and said some things I can't repeat. She was devastated. I still remember her yelling, "Why, why would you do that, your beautiful hair!" The next thing she said was, "Tomorrow we will go to the wig store and get you a wig." My mom was the most loving and strong woman I knew. If she said we would get a wig tomorrow, we probably would. The only thing I could think of doing was to walk into my bedroom, close my bedroom door, and climb out of my window, which I did.

I went over to my friend's house and told her I can't go home. That night I slept underneath her bed and around 1 a.m. my friend's mother came into the bedroom, where I was lying under the bed, and whispered to my friend, "Do you know where Steven is? His mother just called here because he never came home." She said no and I slept there the rest of the night.

The next day was a school day, and I was not about to head to school with this crew cut. I sneaked out of my friend's house and went downtown to spend the day until my friends got out of school and I could meet them.

I guess I still had the conversation about getting to the top of buildings in my head because I decided to go into the Howard Building, which had about thirteen floors. I took the elevator to the top floor with no plan on what I was going to do once I got there. Nobody was on the top floor, so I just started looking around. I eventually went into a back room just to rest because I had several hours to kill before school got out.

About fifteen minutes later, I heard the elevator doors open and the voices of two different men speaking to each other. I peeked out of the room I was in and I saw what looked like two painters carrying cans of paint. I heard one of them say they were going to be there all day painting, which freaked me out. The only way out of the back room was through the front room, exactly where these two guys were. I looked around the room and found a closed door in the back. I opened it and walked out to a small roof that jetted out of the main building. Thirteen floors up, this little roof was no help in me escaping this building. I looked up and there was a smokestack sticking out of the wall, and above that was another roof. I assumed it was the rooftop. I went back into the room and saw a ladder. I picked it up to carry it outside and the back of the ladder banged something as I was carrying it, making a loud noise. I froze thinking these two guys must have heard that noise. I waited for about thirty seconds, and no one came into the room I was in. I proceeded to carry out the ladder onto the mini-roof and placed it leaning on the wall next to the smokestack. Without thinking, I climbed the ladder, used the smokestack to help me reach the top of the main roof, and I managed to get onto the roof. If the ladder somehow ever fell backward with me on it, I would have fallen off the roof and down thirteen stories. I had no idea if I could get access to the building through the main roof, but at that point it was my only option.

I reached the rooftop, stood up, and started heading to the other side of the roof where the main door was. As I was running to the door, I glanced over at what was then called the Hospital Trust Building, and almost every window was filled with people waving their arms, moving from one window to the next, and I realized someone in that building must have seen me putting the ladder up and climbing up the side of the building, and now I had a big audience watching me.

I ran fast, the door opened, and I got into the building, got into the elevator, and pressed the button to the main floor. The elevator door opened and as I walked through the lobby to get to the main doors to leave, several policemen and firemen came running past me and heading into the elevator to, I assumed, go up to the roof

ACTING OUT

to look for the lunatic acting like Spiderman on the roof. I never went back into that building or onto its roof again.

There was also a day that my best friend David's older sister hung out with us, and we jumped on the bus and headed downtown. We were still in our phase of the Bionic Woman and pretending to have her strength. We decided to enter the Old Stone Bank Building in downtown Providence. We were very smart because we concocted a story that if we got caught, we would say that we were looking for our little brother who ran away from us. All I remember of the made-up story was he had sandy blond hair and was cute.

Top Floor of the Old Stone Bank Building

We took the elevator up to the top floor and then started exploring, looking for the door to the roof. We eventually found it, opened the door, and walked onto the roof. The roof had at least two levels because I remember climbing a fixed ladder to get to the highest part of the roof. When we got onto the roof I asked my friends if they heard something like a buzzing noise. We ignored it, not realizing the alarm to the building had been activated when we opened the door to the roof.

Within minutes we heard voices and all three of us tried hiding behind this elevated structure on the roof. As expected, we were caught quickly, and all were taken into separate rooms and questioned. We all remained true to our made-up story about our little brother, and after about two hours, they let us go. If the same thing happened today, I don't think we would have been able to get access to the rooftop or any part of the building and I don't think the police would have just allowed us to leave.

SUNDAY ADVENTURES was always my favorite activity of the week. My same two best friends would come to my house, and we would leave for the day, never sure what trouble we would encounter or create. There was Mount Pleasant Baptist Church on Academy Avenue (I believe it's still there) that had its service at 10 a.m. The church was just several streets over from where we lived. They always had a coffee hour after mass, around 11 a.m., once the service was completed. It included coffee, juice, and pastries. The three of us had taken a Bible Class one summer at the church and I still remember the last song we sang to our parents when the class ended: "Untold millions are still untold, untold millions are outside the fold."

Because we knew the layout of the church, we would swing by around 10:30 a.m. Sunday mornings, head to the basement as the service was going on upstairs, grab some pastries, and continue our adventure.

A couple of blocks from there was Pleasant Valley Parkway. There was a strip of land running down the middle of the street with a little creek running through the island. This is usually where we would sit and eat the pastries we took from the church. One fun thing we would do was to throw sticks into the creek and follow them as they flowed down the water. At one point, the creek ran underground through a tunnel. One day we got the nerve up to follow our sticks into the tunnel and found a table and couch inside. We did see a rat scamper across the tunnel and that was enough for me to run as fast as I could to get out of there. I never went through the tunnel again.

IN OUR NEIGHBORHOOD, there was a three-story house with an older gentleman who owned the house and lived on the second floor. He was very strange but very intriguing to us as teenagers. He would stare out his window for what felt like hours or neighbors would see him and say hi and he would scuffle along with a quick acknowledgment. For many years there were tenants that lived on the first floor, and I believe they were his family. They moved out and he lived in this big house by himself.

Because of his eccentric personality, we assumed he must be a ghost or talk to ghosts. One day the three of us waited for him to leave his house so we could do something crazy: go into his house. However, we couldn't just go in, we needed to take a tape recorder with us and tape the entire adventure. I believe my friend's older sister still has this tape. We were never interested in stealing anything, we just wanted to see the ghosts that we knew were in that house. We entered the door to the basement because the door opened, and we walked right in. Once through the basement, we found the stairs to walk up to the first floor. We also got up into the attic but couldn't access the second floor where he lived because the doors were locked.

As we were walking through the first floor, we heard someone on the second floor walking across the room above us. How could that be possible if the only man who lived in the house was not there? It had to be the ghost! The three of us ran as fast as we could out of the house and didn't stop until we were significantly away from the house. I sometimes think of him and wish I knew more about him.

MY OTHER BEST FRIEND Paul and I met in my freshman year of high school. We are still best friends today and talk, text, or email each other several times a day. Paul was very quiet in high school and in senior year the dean of students walked by him, stopped, stared, and asked if he was new to the school. Paul attended the school for four years. The dean of students knew me very well because I was always in trouble.

From taking the fire extinguisher off the wall and spraying students as they entered the hallway, to running as fast as I could and body-slamming a large filing cabinet, enough to leave a very big dent in it.

In my second year of high school, we started our second semester around November. That semester our religion class was going to be focused on substance abuse prevention and it was taught by one of the priests. One of my friends had a friend he grew up with who was also in school with us. I was aware that he liked smoking marijuana and he invited me to smoke after school, which I declined. Then I got this great idea. I went to his locker one day when classes were being held and searched for a joint in his locker. I found one. Most likely a lot of students would have taken that joint and smoked it, but I never was inclined to do drugs. It wasn't my thing. So, what did I do with it? I went early to the classroom where our religious class was taught, and I dropped the joint into the priest's coffee cup that was sitting on his desk. The cup was empty.

The class was filled with all the students and Paul was also in that class. The priest walked in, ready to start the semester on drugs, noticed his coffee cup with the joint in it, and started screaming. I have never seen someone's face get so red in my life. I could see the spit shooting out of his mouth as he continuously yelled, "Who did this, who did this?" Nobody except Paul knew I did it and of course, I never admitted to it.

The principal and the dean of students did come to the classroom and warned all of us that any individual would be automatically expelled from the school if they ever did something like that again. Many years later, with Paul with me, I told my mother I did that. I just remember her shaking her head in disbelief. She always told people that she wished her oldest boy was like her youngest, he is an angel, and never gets in trouble. I didn't get in trouble because I was good at getting away with things. As a matter of fact, someone recently said to me, "You have an angelic face." Things haven't changed much.

I hated going to the gym especially when gym class was one of the first classes. I already had my hair exactly the way I wanted it and getting sweaty in the gym was going to ruin all my hard work. During sophomore year I came up with an idea. I wanted to have another friend write a note stating I couldn't participate in gym class because I had tendonitis in the ankles and wrists. He signed the note as a doctor and the paper he used was colored paper from the drugstore. It wasn't an official paper and there was no doctor's name or address printed on it. I was so nervous handing the note to the gym teacher with the explanation I just went to the doctor because my wrists and ankles were bothering me. To my surprise, it worked! When I received my report card for the following semester, under GYM instead of saying Pass or Fail it said "ME" for a medical excuse.

When my mom asked me about it, I simply told her you either get ME for meeting expectations or F for failing. She looked like she believed me and for the following two years of high school, I never went to the gym again. Junior year I wanted Paul to be with me in the library, where I would go during gym class, and I knew he hated gym also. I told him I could get a note for him too, so he didn't have to take the gym class. After working with him for days, he agreed. Junior year he was recovering from a broken arm so he couldn't take gym, and senior year he became anemic so also couldn't take gym. At least that is what the notes said. It was so nice having him with me in the library!

Senior year all the students had to do a certain number of hours of community service to be able to graduate. I was assigned to work at the Franciscan Order, which was not too far from my house. We would do community service on Saturdays, and I was not thrilled. The first Saturday I showed up, one of the nuns told me they needed the floor washed and waxed. She showed me where the bucket, mop, and wax were and left me alone. I realized at some point if you mix the cleaning solution with the wax solution, the floor becomes extremely slippery. I began to run across the floor and slide, crashing into chairs and anything that was on the perimeter of the floor. I went a little too fast and hit the table which made a loud noise. Two nuns came into the room and started yelling at me. They told me to clean the mess up that I made and when I was done, told me to leave and never go back there again.

Paul's community service was painting the inside of a building and he continuously told me I must find another place to do community service, or I will not graduate. I never did, and I strongly believe that the reason I graduated without the community service certificate was they just wanted me out of that school. I remember the day when the dean of students, whom everyone was petrified of, said to me, "In twenty-five years being at this school, I have never seen a student cause so much disruption in four years, and that statement is being generous."

MY COLLEGE YEARS were interesting, to say the least. After I graduated from high school, I had to go to college whether I wanted to or not. Those were my mother's words. She always wanted the best for her two sons. I decided to go to the University of Rhode Island and the campus was about forty-five minutes from my home. The thought of living on campus never crossed my mind. After my dad passed away, I dealt with anxiety, and living away from home was too overwhelming. A neighborhood friend, Karen, luckily was also going to attend URI and was planning to commute. She had a car, so on most days I would commute with her to school. Driving with Karen was a lot of fun because we talked about childhood memories and experiences we encountered as kids.

ACTING OUT

After about the first month of school, the desire to attend classes was waning. I remember, in my Marketing class, I received the highest grade on our first test. The ironic thing is, I never attended that class afterward. I hated school. I would walk around campus, sit in Karen's car, or just explore the surrounding area as I waited for Karen to finish her classes.

One day, I entered a building on campus that I had never been to before. It appeared to be a theater. I entered through the back door, and I could hear voices coming from the front of the building. I looked to my left and saw two large mats. They were thick, flat mats; ones you would use for gymnastics. Growing up, I did gymnastics all the time. I did take lessons, but that didn't last too long because I never felt comfortable in large crowds. I just loved doing gymnastics in my yard with friends. One summer, I choreographed a routine that included cartwheels, back walkovers, splits, and much more. I was very proud of that routine.

With winter approaching, I thought it would be great to have those mats in my house to be able to practice gymnastics during the winter. I grabbed the bigger one and dragged it across the floor and through the doorway. I continued dragging the mat through the parking lot until I got to Karen's car. It took me a while, but I eventually fit it in the back seat of the car.

Once that was done, I went back in for the smaller mat and did the same thing. When Karen was done with her classes, I saw her walking up to the car with a confused look on her face. She asked me where the mats came from, and I told her they were throwing them out, so I took them. We then headed home. The second-floor tenants at my mom's house had moved out by then, so I put the mats up there and used them quite frequently practicing gymnastics. Once my mom saw them, I told her the same story that I told Karen, and she believed me.

As the year progressed, I would try to persuade Karen not to go to class. Sometimes it worked and we either went to breakfast or to the pond to feed ducks or to the stables to see the horses. I never told my mother that I wasn't going to school. I would leave our house each day to go to campus and she worked full time, so if I got home earlier she had no idea what time I arrived back at the house.

My mom received social security benefits for my brother and me due to our father passing away. Once we turned eighteen, the benefits would stop unless we continued to college full time. After the first year of college was over, my mom received a letter from social security stating her son did not attend college full time, therefore she was not eligible for the monthly benefits. At that point, I had to tell her the truth that I hadn't attended classes since last October. My mom had no idea, so she completed the form social security sent her attesting I was a full-time college student. The government then decided that the amount my mom received during the previous school year needed to be reimbursed to social security. Because I was no longer a minor, the responsibility was on me to pay it back. For the following seven or eight years, every tax refund I had coming to me was intercepted by the government to pay back the total amount. Every year I would receive a letter stating my refund was taken to pay down the existing debt. I was so happy the first year I received my tax refund, and the debt was completely paid off.

Because I was not attending school, I needed to get a full-time job. I had several jobs and one of them was working for People's Bank in the mortgage department in downtown Providence. I met a woman named Deanna in my department and we instantly became friends. One day we went to lunch, as we always did, and when we got back we were about four minutes over the time allocated for lunch. Our supervisor came out of her office and started reprimanding us both about being back late from lunch. At that moment, I realized these would be the types of jobs I would have without having a college degree and I knew that wasn't going to work for me. That night I got home and told my mom I think I want to go back to school full time and work part time and she was thrilled. I know she thought that would be another four years living at home, which made her very happy. Did I mention I have the best mother in the world?

Throughout college, I worked three part-time jobs: at a bank, Jordan Marsh department store, and Tanorama, a tanning salon with stand-up chambers. When I interviewed at Jordan Marsh, I assumed I would be on the floor as a salesperson. When I mentioned I was attending college for accounting, the person interviewing me asked if I would be interested in working in the credit department because they had an opening. I said yes and met the credit department manager who was very nice. I worked in the credit department for six years and loved the people I worked with. Back then, the salespeople would promote opening a Jordan Marsh credit card to their customers. If they were successful, they would bring the completed applications up to the credit department and we would put a white circle sticker on their sheet. Once they received ten stickers, they would get a scratch ticket. They could win money or a percentage off a purchase.

One Saturday evening I was on my break at work and I took a walk in the mall. Jordan Marsh was part of Warwick Mall in Warwick, Rhode Island. As I was coming back to the credit department, I noticed in the women's dress department a navy blue dress with white polka dots on it. The white dots were the same size as the circle stickers we gave out to salespeople. When the store was closed, the credit department staff would walk out with the management who was working that night. I was working with Carolyn, a woman who was in her forties and someone I adored. As the managers were walking ahead of us, right when we got to the rack of the blue polka dot dresses,

I pulled out a couple of sheets with the circle stickers on them and told Carolyn these dots are the same size dots on the dress so let's put more dots on some dresses.

At first, she looked at me and said, "No, we can't do that." After I started placing the white dot stickers on a dress, she motioned with her open hand and said to give her a sheet. We used up all the dot stickers by randomly picking several of the polka-dot dresses and placing the stickers on those dresses. When we were done, we caught up to the managers and they didn't even realize we weren't walking behind them the entire time.

Several weeks later I was working on a Saturday afternoon. Saturday afternoon had the most people working in the credit department because the three ladies that would count the week's deposits were in the back, and there were usually three or four people working on the front line taking care of customers. Suddenly, we heard a woman yelling in the next office. The office next to the credit department was the executive office. After a couple of minutes of her voice getting loud and then quiet, the door swung open, and she came barreling out of the executive office appearing to be quite upset.

One of the floor supervisors, Jo, came into the credit department and all of us were asking what that was about. Jo said this crazy woman came in and was complaining that a dress with polka dots she purchased had the dots falling off the dress and they weren't real dots. Of course, Jo and all of us started laughing but nobody but Carolyn and I knew that we put the dots on the dresses. Carolyn was working that afternoon and would not look at me. When I finally got to chat with her privately, we laughed so much that our stomachs hurt. We never told anyone in the credit department that we had done that but each of us told our family and friends. What a great story!

INSIGHT

Believing and trusting that there is an afterlife is mandatory to connect with spirit. One thing I've learned is there is a difference between saying you believe in spirit and actually believing it. After my father passed away, I know I had spirit guiding me, watching me, and most importantly, protecting me and keeping me safe. That would not have changed if I didn't believe in the afterlife, however, it would have made it so much more difficult for me to connect with spirit once I realized I was a Medium. Every part of your being must believe in spirit. This is not easy due to most of the spirit world not being something tangible or something you can physically see. Start repeating to yourself that the afterlife is real and just because you can't physically see spirit, doesn't mean spirit doesn't exist. The more you state that your loved ones, who have crossed over are still here, the more the door that separates us from spirit starts opening.

CHAPTER 03

COMING OUT

W hen I met my best friend Paul in my first year in high school, if sexuality came up at all it would be a conversation about a girl. The conversations were never long. When I met the first guy I started dating, I was dying to talk to someone about what I was feeling for him. I remember one warm August evening going over to Paul's house. In the summer, all of his family would stay at their beach house except for Paul, who chose to stay home. We sat at his kitchen table and I told him there was something I needed to tell him, but it wasn't easy for me to talk about. I then said, "If you want me to leave as soon as I tell you, I completely understand." After stumbling with words for a few minutes, I got up the courage to say, "I am gay, and I am dating a guy." I was sweating and nervous because I had no idea what his response would be.

The next thing I heard was, "I am gay too." We stared at each other for a couple of seconds and then exploded with laughter and questions. It was a night I will never forget. As a matter of fact, right before I got up the nerve to tell Paul, he lost electricity and the house went dark. There were thunderstorms moving through and Paul grabbed some candles and lit them so we could see and continue our conversation. Only two gay guys would have such a theatrical coming out with wind, thunder, and candlelight.

MY FIRST LOVE was my first in many aspects. Going through college, as mentioned, I had three jobs. On my breaks at Jordan Marsh, I would walk around the mall to shop or grab something to eat. I used to walk by this guy frequently who worked at a sunglasses store in the mall, and one day as I was passing by, he said, "hi." I said hi and stopped to look at sunglasses with no intention of buying a pair; I just wanted to talk to him. Eventually, we started dating. It was my first relationship with a guy as previously I dated girls and they were always short-lived flings. Two days after I met him, I had my first date with him. He picked me up at my house and we headed to the east side of Providence to find a restaurant to get something to eat.

We stopped at a red light in Olneyville, a section of Providence, and he spontaneously leaned over and kissed me. The light turned green, and he continued driving. It was a moment I will never forget. He was my first love. After we ate, we parked near the bay and did a lot of kissing. When he eventually dropped me back at my house, I just replayed what happened over and over again in my head. I finally knew what butterflies in your stomach felt like.

A couple of months later, I bought my first new car. It was a red Pontiac LeMans and I was very excited. One night, the two of us drove up to Boston to go to some clubs there. It is about a fifty-minute ride from Providence to Boston. On our return, I was driving home at about 2 a.m. on the highway. The exit on the highway I would have been taking in Providence to go home was the next exit, but I fell asleep before I made it there. I closed my eyes for a couple of seconds and when I opened my eyes, the driver's side of the car was climbing up the median that separates the two lanes, and I realized that I lost control of the car.

The car then flipped over five times, sliding across all four lanes of the highway, knocked down the exit sign, and eventually stopped once it hit a giant bush and the impact caused the car to spin in a circle several times. All the windows except the back window were blown out and the roof looked like a dented can of vegetables. The firefighters and EMTs could not understand how the roof didn't collapse and kill both of us. My then-boyfriend had some glass in his eye that was washed out on the scene and he was fine. The car went a significant distance on its roof and the friction of the cement street and roof tore a hole in the roof above the driver's seat. I was holding my head away from the roof as much as possible and using my shoulder to lean on the roof. The friction started to rip my leather jacket on the shoulder and ultimately the jacket was ruined. I was very upset about the jacket because I had just purchased it about one month ago.

When I was experiencing these incidents, I never thought about a higher power or if I had any help from another dimension. Occasionally, I would think about my father being around and wonder if he helped me in certain circumstances, but that was always a fleeting thought. However, the feeling that somehow I was magical never left me.

After dating for about nine months, one night we were bored and decided to drive up to Boston to go to some bars. We settled in this one bar and at some point, he asked me to go to the bathroom with him. I followed him into the bathroom, and he entered one of the bathroom stalls and motioned me to follow him into the stall. I naively thought he wanted to make out but that wasn't his intention. He pulled a vial out of his pocket and gently started shaking a white substance on top of the toilet paper dispenser. He then bent forward so his head was adjacent to the dispenser and holding one nostril shut, he sniffed some of that white substance into his nose.

This was the first time I had ever been exposed to cocaine and when I realized what it was, it scared me. He then said to take some and started showing me exactly the method to inhale the cocaine. I remember saying "no way" and immediately opening the stall door and walking out of the stall and the bathroom. Again, doing drugs was never something I was interested in and frankly it just seemed ridiculous to do. After about ten minutes, the realization hit me: I am dating someone who does cocaine.

When the cocaine incident occurred, it startled me and I never saw it coming. As I thought about our relationship, things started making more sense. He used to stop at this random house and ask me to stay in the car because he just needed to run in and drop something off to a friend. I never saw any evidence of him doing drugs, but there were several times he would go to the bathroom and come back in a different mood or act tipsy like he drank more liquor than he had.

He was my first love, but I knew the relationship could not continue after experiencing the bathroom stall incident. As heartbreaking as it was, I decided I needed to break up with him. The conversation was not easy to bring up and he did not take it well. He cried, I cried, and after about two hours I left his house and we had broken up, or so I thought.

A couple of days later I came home from work and my aunt was sitting in the kitchen with my mom. My mom had a very serious look on her face and almost immediately after I entered the kitchen, she said, "Your friend came over today and said that he was your boyfriend, and he didn't understand why you broke up with him." I was shocked and never expected that conversation to occur. I vehemently denied it and told my mom and aunt that I found out he was doing cocaine and that is why I ended our friendship. I told them he is not in his right mind and very upset that I don't want to see him anymore, so he came here and made up this story.

I obviously never had a conversation with my mom about being gay, but when I was ready for that conversation, I wanted it to be initiated by me and not by an ex-boyfriend. My mom always knew I was gay. I am sure she never wanted to acknowledge it and maybe hoped someday I would meet a nice girl and get married. However, I would spend every second of my day with him. He would sleep over at my house, in my bedroom with me, sharing the same bed, probably several times a week. Two young straight guys who are best friends share a lot of things, but they don't share a bed several times a week.

About two months after we broke up, my best friend David and I, who passed away in 1997, went to a video bar called The Fan Club in Providence. We sat at the bar, and I noticed the bartender was very handsome. I remember David turning to me and saying, "The bartender just replaced your drink with a new one without you asking him for another one." I thanked the bartender and found out his name was Eric, and he owned the Fan Club. We talked for a while and before I left, we exchanged phone numbers. We went out on a couple of dates and one night we decided to meet at Mirabar, a gay bar, for a drink. When we left the bar, I went to my car and Eric went to his car. We parked at opposite ends of the parking lot, so I never saw him again that night. When I reached my car, I found my ex-boyfriend leaning on my car. He started asking me who was the guy I was with at Mirabar and several other questions. I told him to go home, and I attempted to open my car door to get into the car. He wrapped his arms around me and begged to get back together. I tried to get out of his grip and we both lost our balance and fell to the ground. We both got up, he yelled at me in anger, and he jumped into his car and took off. I got into my car but noticed something was wrong with my left arm. I didn't have control of it anymore. I started to shake as I knew something was very wrong.

I drove home and went into my house and headed right into my bedroom. It was about 2 a.m. so my mom was sleeping, and I don't think my brother was home at that time. I jumped into bed and prayed that my arm would be ok when I woke up in the morning. I reached over to the arm that I didn't have control over and laid it on my chest and went to sleep. I woke up early, around 7 a.m., and unfortunately, my arm was no better. As I got out of bed, it just hung to the side of me. I walked into the kitchen where my mom was sitting at the table having breakfast and said to her in tears, "I think my arm is broken."

My mom and brother asked me what happened, so I told them. Immediately, my brother wanted to find my ex-boyfriend and "have a talk with him." I talked him out of that plan. Ultimately, the three of us went to the ER. The doctor confirmed my suspicion that my arm was broken and immediately started talking about surgery once the swelling went down. I was never so scared in my life.

*Taking it easy with
a broken arm*

My mom found another doctor for a second opinion, with a great reputation. He told us there was an extremely small chance that my arm would heal by itself in a cast, but he was willing to try if we insisted on taking that route, which we did. I wore a hard cast for about two-and-a-half-months and luckily it was summer, so I did manage to get myself to the beach, cast and all, weekly. Miraculously my arm healed by itself without surgery, but I know I had help from spirit to get me to that result.

I never saw Eric again after my broken arm incident, and was devastated when about one year after we dated, I got the news that he died of AIDS. I have always thanked god and every spirit connected to me that I managed to avoid contracting HIV. So many beautiful gay souls succumbed to this disease, but thankfully the treatment now is so effective. I send white light, healing, and love to all those beautiful gay men in spirit.

In the following year, I dated a lot. I was finally living the true life I was given and having a lot of fun living that life. At that point, I still hadn't had a conversation with my mom about me being gay but if I brought a guy to my house that she didn't know, she would barely say anything to me until the guy left the house. I continued dating, she never brought anything up about me being gay, and we both moved forward.

THE NIGHT I MET MY SOULMATE On April 8, 1993, my friend Glenn and I went to Boston to this upscale club called Club Cafe. I met Glenn at Mirabar in Providence and realized we both worked at Jordan Marsh. He worked on the floor as a salesman. We became very good friends and are still friends today.

Club Cafe is divided into the restaurant in the front and the bar and video room/lounge in the back. Glenn and I were scanning the room for cute guys when I saw this guy talking to another guy. He had olive skin, dark hair, and dressed nicely, and when he smiled my heart dropped to my feet. I could not keep my eyes off him. I watched him walk away from the guy he was talking to and head into the adjoining room where the bar was located. To this day, I have no idea why I did this, but I walked up to the back of him and reached out my hand and pushed him gently on his back. He quickly turned around with an annoyed look on his face to see me just smiling at him.

The year we met, 1993, and I had no idea I created this heart with my hands until many years later!

While still smiling, I said hi and I told him my name. He said his name was Elix and smiled back. Immediately I noticed he had an accent and I asked him where he was from. He told me about Puerto Rico and asked me if I had ever been there. I told him no and we stayed in the same spot for about ten minutes chatting. I was so excited talking to him. At some point, Elix said to me, "I wish I could keep on talking to you but I'm on a date and have to get back to him." I was deflated and when I got back to Glenn, I told him this guy is just a player; he's on another date and is a jerk.

However, afterward, I kept my eyes on Elix, watching exactly where he was and what he was doing. At some point, I scanned the room, and he was gone. I was so disappointed. After Elix left, a handsome guy approached me and started a conversation. He was in law school, which is ironic because, in four years, I would be starting law school. He asked me if I wanted another drink, I said no, and he said he was going to the bar and would be right back. I was standing there waiting for his return when I turned to the right towards the long hallway leading out of the restaurant and saw Elix walking directly toward me. Elix came right up to me, and I asked him where his date was. Elix told me he put him in a taxi because he wasn't feeling well and sent him home. I vaguely remember the law student coming back to resume our conversation, but I was so involved in the conversation with Elix, at some point he disappeared for good.

The remaining time was spent chatting with Elix and before I left the club, we exchanged phone numbers, and the entire ride home I was on cloud nine. Within the next couple of days, we went on our first date. He lived in Massachusetts, and I was living in Rhode Island, so he drove down and I took him to the East Side in Providence for dinner. A friend of mine, Donna, was working at a restaurant in Providence and told me to swing by for dessert so she could check him out. We had a wonderful dinner and then I took him for dessert to the restaurant where Donna worked. At one

COMING OUT

point, Elix went to the bathroom and Donna ran over to me and said, "Oh my god, he is so handsome, and I love his accent." She highly approved of him and loves him still today, and the feelings are mutual.

A couple of weeks after we started dating, Elix called and asked me if I wanted to see him that night, and he was willing to drive down to see me. I told him I was tired and not feeling one 100 percent, so we decided to speak the next day. Moments after that call, my friend Glenn called me to tell me he and three other friends were going to Boston to go clubbing and to get ready. I told him I was tired and just wanted to stay home. A couple of minutes later, two of my friends called me and begged me to go. I ultimately changed my mind and decided to go.

We drove up to Boston and went to a gay club and we were having a great time dancing and laughing, and then someone walked by me, and he was passing out glow sticks. I took a bunch of them, and they were all connected. You are supposed to separate them and then bend them so the liquid inside becomes activated and the sticks start glowing. I did bend them, but I did not separate them. I got a great idea to put them in my pants starting from one ankle, going up one leg, crossing over my crotch, and going down the other leg. The result was having glow sticks in my pants and the front of my legs glowing through my jeans. It wasn't easy but I managed to get one long connected glow in my pants. I was on the dance floor, getting so much attention from people laughing and pointing at the glow sticks in my pants, and then I saw Glenn come running onto the dance floor heading straight to me with a serious expression on his face.

Glenn grabbed my arm and said, "Elix is here in the club." I panicked, remembering I told him earlier I was tired and just wanted to stay home. As I was heading off the dance floor, I was simultaneously trying to pull the glow sticks out of my pants. In the middle of trying to do both, I looked up and Elix was in front of me, just staring. In a very serious tone, he asked if he could talk to me. He told me he wasn't into games and that if I wasn't serious about dating, this wasn't going to work out. I tried my best to explain the situation and I think he believed me. A situation like that never happened again and on April 8, 2023, we celebrated thirty years of being together. It has been the best thirty years of my life.

Since Elix lived almost an hour away in another state, I was spending more and more time with him in his apartment and not in my house where I lived with my mom. Our relationship got stronger as we dated, and I knew that I had found my forever person. My mother was not thrilled that I was spending more time at Elix's apartment. If it was up to her, I would live in her house forever and she would be very content.

INTRODUCING ELIX TO MY MOTHER was not what I expected. My nephew, Tristan, was born on September 11, 1991. My brother had been living in New York City since before my nephew was born. This was my mom's first grandchild, so she was ecstatic about Tristan. My mother wanted to have Tristan's christening celebration in her home in Rhode Island because all of the family was there so it would be more convenient for travel. My mom and brother agreed on a date in August of 1993.

I asked Elix to come to my house so he could meet my mom, brother, and the rest of the family. Elix arrived at my house, and I opened the door to greet him. I introduced him to my mother; she was very cordial to him and said it was nice to meet him. She immediately grabbed her car keys, with a house full of people for a party that she was hosting, jumped in her car, and left the party. My brother didn't realize she left until I told him. He was in disbelief that she had just left, but I told him it was because I asked Elix to come to the party and I was sorry this situation happened.

Shortly after that Elix and I left and went back to his apartment. It was very sad that I missed most of my nephew's christening, but I thought it was the right decision at the time. She eventually came back, and I am not sure how many people realized what happened, or that she had left the party. Every year in September, there is the world's only multi-state fair, the Eastern States Exposition (the Big E), which occurs for two weeks in Springfield, Massachusetts. I had been going there for years with my family as it was always an annual event for us. It was September 1994, and I found out my mother was taking the bus to the fair and my brother and family were driving up from New York City to meet there. I decided that Elix and I would also go so we could have another chance of seeing my family. I was hoping my mother would be open to seeing Elix and be more accepting of who he was to me. I also asked my friend Jacqui, whom I worked with at the time, to come along.

We all picked a time and place to meet at the fair and I was very nervous walking toward that location to see my family. My mother, brother, his wife, and my nephew, who was three years old at the time, were there. I introduced my family again to Elix, and also to Jacqui. The meeting only lasted a couple of minutes, but my mother never said one word to Elix; she acted like he wasn't there. Ironically, she did acknowledge Jacqui. My brother and his wife were very nice to Elix and chatted with him. I was so angry with my mother after we left, but also so sad because I knew how bad Elix felt after that interaction, or lack thereof, from my mother.

For Christmas, 1993, Elix and I spent it apart. I was with my family and Elix went to Puerto Rico to spend the holidays with his family. In 1994, I asked my mom if Elix could come to our house for Christmas and she said no. I believe that was the defining moment for both of us. I spent Christmas Eve, 1994, with Elix in his apartment, and on Christmas Day I went to my mother's house, dropped off gifts, and said I was leaving. She was hosting Christmas dinner at her house and the extended family was going there.

She got very upset, and I told her Elix was a very important part of my life and he wasn't going anywhere. If she did not want to associate with him, the time spent between us would decrease. She didn't say too much, and I left and spent Christmas day with Elix.

It took her a couple of months after that to realize she didn't want our relationship to change or for us not to see each other as much as we always did. In Rhode Island, there is an annual tradition called May Breakfast. Many restaurants and churches celebrate May Breakfast or May Day (May 1) by offering special breakfasts. In May 1995 the church in my neighborhood, St. Peter's and St. Andrew's Episcopal Church, was having a May Breakfast. I had been going to that church for May Breakfast since I was a little boy. I called my mom and told her I was going to breakfast with Elix and my best friend David, and we would be there at 8 a.m. I assumed she would then wait to go after 9 a.m. so she didn't have to interact with Elix.

The three of us were sitting and having breakfast when David, who was facing the door said, "Steven, your mother just walked in." My body tensed up worrying if she was going to make a commotion when she saw the three of us there together. She walked up to our table, said hi to all of us, including Elix, sat with us, and talked to Elix like she had been talking to him for years. Their relationship progressively got stronger and stronger over the years, and she absolutely loved him like another son. The three of us did something every weekend and I thank god that the situation was resolved in the best possible manner.

MY FIRST SIGN? Elix and I were heading down to Providence, Rhode Island to pick up my mom from her house and take her to dinner. We arrived and walked up the pathway to her back door and went inside. My mom was almost all ready to go, so Elix said he was heading outside to wait for us. About one minute later, I followed Elix and walked outside.

I opened the back door and stepped out. I started walking down the pathway to the car when I noticed a blue balloon sitting there. Elix was sitting at the other end of the sidewalk waiting for us, so I asked him where the balloon came from. He said when he walked down the pathway minutes ago, that balloon wasn't there. I picked it up and it was clear that someone blew into it to blow it up because when I dropped it, it fell to the ground. My mom came out of the house and saw me holding the balloon. Instead of commenting on the balloon, she looked at me and said, "I meant to remind you that today is Daddy's anniversary." I looked back at her and said "Imagine if Daddy put this balloon here for us to see because it is his anniversary."

I do not know why I did this, but I told my mom and Elix to go with me to the larger part of the yard. They followed me and on the way to the bigger part of the yard, the balloon slipped out of my hand and fell to the ground. I picked it up and continued walking. With the three of us in the yard I said, "Dad if you sent this to us, I am sending it back." Holding the balloon in my hand, I raised that arm and let go of the balloon. As if someone grabbed the balloon from me, filled it with helium, then put it back in my hand, the balloon flew up into the sky. In amazement, we watched this balloon heading to the clouds and eventually it got so high, we could no longer see it.

The rest of the day my mind was confused. How could that have happened? I dropped it twice and it fell to the ground. How was it possible that this balloon could fly into the sky? Was it really my dad? Did he give me my first sign? I loved believing this was him, but thought nothing like this would ever happen again. I knew this experience would hold a dear place in my heart.

INSIGHT

Being authentic. I am not sure when I realized I was gay, probably when I was about ten years old. I knew there was something different about me at an early age, but I am not sure I was able to label it prior to being about ten or eleven years old. There were many years I pretended to be straight. It was one of the hardest things I ever had to do and I didn't realize how that facade affected every aspect of my life. You must be one 100 percent accepting of yourself and live an authentic life to be able to fully connect with your soul and spirit. Wearing masks may protect you from owning who you are, but those masks also prevent a strong connection between you and your universe. Being proud and happy about the person you are is mandatory to not only connect with your soul and spirit, but to hone in on the particular way you connect with spirit.

CHAPTER 04

PUERTO RICO

Almost all of Elix's family was living in Puerto Rico when I met him. Elix came to the United States to go to college, and he attained his bachelor's and master's degrees from Emerson College. He asked me to come to Puerto Rico for the holidays in December 1993 to meet his family and see where he grew up. I had already met his mom in May 1993. Unlike my mom, she acted very friendly to me; maybe that was because she spoke Spanish mostly and I didn't speak Spanish. She did complain to the immediate family that she wasn't happy Elix was with me, but that changed fairly quickly and we have a wonderful relationship. She lives with us in our in-law's apartment and is ninety-seven years old.

I slept over at my best friend's house in Rhode Island the night before I left for Puerto Rico so he could take me to the airport in the morning. There was a snowstorm that started the night before and it was snowing heavily the next morning when I was leaving for Puerto Rico. Paul took me to the airport, and I was praying the flight was not going to be canceled. I just wanted to see Elix. Despite several airlines canceling flights, mine was not canceled. I can still picture the pink liquid dripping down the windows of the plane as I sat inside. Right before we took off, the plane needed to be de-iced. It didn't matter to me. I was going to Puerto Rico to see Elix and nothing was going to stop me.

On the plane to Puerto Rico, I met a woman named Iran. We started chatting only minutes before the plane landed in Puerto Rico and she led me to the part of the airport where I needed to retrieve my luggage. She was so friendly and told me how much I would love the island and I would have a great time.

Elix was waiting for me at ground transportation and gave me the biggest hug to greet me and welcome me to his Island. I told him all about Iran and he told me that Iran is not a girl's name and asked if I was sure I was talking to a girl. I laughed and said I know the difference between a guy and a girl, and to this day Elix jokes that Iran was a guy.

Right after we left the airport, Elix took me to San Juan. We walked around and I was surprised at how much of a metropolitan city it was. I never heard a lot about Puerto Rico so I didn't realize San Juan would look like any other big city. I also loved the weather. As we strolled through San Juan, I was still thinking about how nervous I was to meet his family. Elix told me that for Three Kings Day the entire family goes to the **Campo** to celebrate. The **Campo** was the family's house in the mountains. Elix has a big family. His dad is one of thirteen and his mom is one of seven. His grandmother was the matriarch of the family, and she was the center of the celebration on January 6th. I was the most nervous about meeting her.

When we pulled up to Elix's family's house, I immediately heard dogs barking in the backyard. We walked into the house, and I was greeted by his mom, Consuelo, and then introduced to his dad, Servando. Elix's mom spoke a little bit of English to me, but his dad only spoke Spanish. We stayed at his parents' home in one of the spare bedrooms. The next morning, I was awakened by the calls of a rooster. Elix's parent's home has a very big and long backyard. There are a lot of trees and bushes and somewhere back there were his dad's chickens, a rooster, and several dogs.

I quickly learned Elix's dad's daily routine. He would be in the backyard with the animals starting at 6 a.m. or earlier, come into the house around 2 p.m., take a shower, get dressed, and leave for his job at the Cash & Carry. He would arrive back home at around 9 p.m. Consuelo would wait for Servo to get home to eat, and many times I saw them eating off the same plate. It was one of the cutest things I have ever seen.

Three Kings Day is extremely festive in Puerto Rico. Elix made plans with one of his best friends in Puerto Rico, Mandy, to go to this club the night before Three Kings Day. Elix and I stopped to pick Mandy up at his house and when we went inside, Mandy's mom was sitting in the living room and was very friendly. Then Mandy came out of his bedroom, and I was introduced to him. Elix and Mandy had many stories about growing up in Puerto Rico, and I had the pleasure of hearing many fond memories on the ride to the club.

Mandy was diagnosed with ALS several years ago and passed away about two years after his diagnosis. Fortunately, we were able to see him many times after his diagnosis when we were visiting Puerto Rico. The last visit, he was in a nursing home and unable to move any part of his body, but he still had such a wonderful sense of humor. That loss was very hard for Elix.

Mandy had a couple of friends meet us at the club that night before Three Kings Day, and I remember one of his friends looked identical to the Latin singer John Secada. All his friends were very nice, and we had a great time. I do remember driving home and before we got to Elix's parents' house, you could see dawn was not far away. I knew we had to get up early to head to the **Campo** so I tried to get as much sleep in a short period of time as I could.

The drive to the **Campo** was beautiful. We were surrounded by mountains and palm trees, and it felt as if the car was going uphill forever. Some parts were a little treacherous because it was a dirt road with no barriers on the outside of the road. Looking on one side of the road showed you how high up we were.

When we arrived, there were already family members there. There was a long driveway leading up to the house and it was surrounded by palm trees, orange trees, grapefruit trees, etc. It was breathtaking. Music was playing and the next hour or so was just a constant number of family members arriving at the house.

Elix, some of his cousins, and I decided to take a walk through the mountains. It was like strolling in a rainforest with brooks running through the mountains, and flowers everywhere; it was a gorgeous sight. One cousin took a bag with her and filled the bag with oranges and grapefruits as we continued our adventure. When we returned to the house, her bag was completely full. I have no idea how she carried that bag.

At one point, we came across a little house much higher in the mountains than Elix's family's house. The father, mother, and three children all came out of the house to greet us. Of course, they were speaking Spanish but offered us water and were so nice to us. We then headed back down to the house.

When we returned, the smell of food was everywhere, and it smelled so good. Elix introduced me to one of his cousins and seconds later, she grabbed me, pulled me into the center of the driveway, and started dancing with me. It was an incredible party with nothing but dancing, laughing, and eating.

When the food was ready to eat, one of Elix's uncles, who was fluent in English, sat next to me. We started talking and then I realized he was eating something that was crunchy. I asked him what he was eating, and he said a part of the pig's ear. I jumped up and ran to find Elix to tell him what his uncle just told me. Elix started laughing and when the food was served, I only ate salad and rice.

When it was time to meet Elix's grandmother, Elix brought me to her. Elix introduced us and she spoke to me in English. She had beautiful blue eyes and immediately I knew she liked me (thank god)! We spoke for a couple of minutes and then she said something to a family member in Spanish and they scurried away. They came back and handed her a bottle. She reached out to me, held my hand, and said she wanted to give me her very special family wine. I was so honored and thanked her. When she handed me the bottle, the label said the family name with a picture of her on it. Elix was shocked as well as so many of his family members that she gave me a bottle of wine after meeting me for the first time. I heard several times that day, "She never gives the wine out to anybody, how did you get that?" I felt so validated and a little cocky. Family members still bring that up to this day. It was a great day.

INSIGHT

There have been many times throughout my life that I have felt like I don't fit in. It is an awful feeling when you tell yourself you are not good enough or less than the environment you are in or the people around you. Once I realized I was a Medium, I finally acknowledged that I was special and that I could do something that most people can't. I should have always known I was special solely because I was born. Feeling I was worthy because I am a Medium was a temporary feeling. It was just another external validation. When you get to the point of waking up in the morning, looking at your reflection in the mirror and smiling, realizing that reflection is a miracle, you then understand the true reason of why you are here.

CHAPTER 05

——◆·◆·◦◯◦·◆·◆——

SETTLING IN

When Elix and I met in 1993, he was working for Blue Cross in Boston, and I was working for Citizens Bank in Rhode Island. I had just graduated from college with a bachelor's in accounting and I worked for several years as a teller at the same bank. After obtaining my degree, I interviewed for a position in the audit department, and I was offered the job. It was so hard leaving the people at the branch; they were like family to me. However, I was very happy to have been given this opportunity.

When I got the job as a teller, I had to attend training with about twenty other people that had just been hired by the bank. On the last day of training, we received our assignments, i.e., which branch we would be working in. Everyone opened their envelopes and stated where they were going. I opened mine up and it said, "Garden City." Someone yelled out in the room "Steven, where are you going?" and I replied I was assigned to Garden City. All I heard from all the trainers was, "Oh," "Omg," or "Good luck!" My eyes opened wide, and I asked what was wrong with Garden City. The trainers all backed down and said it's fine, it's just a little different, a little crazy, you will find out soon enough. I never anticipated what I was in for.

The Garden City branch was known for being unique. A branch that somehow attracted only crazy staff and likable customers, and was not a typical banking environment. After several years of working there, some of the above-mentioned things may be true, but you couldn't find more friendly, caring, compassionate people in any other branch. My assignment to be stationed at Garden City was a perfect choice!

One Friday night, a long-term customer came to one of the drive-up windows and said he had tomatoes from his garden he wanted to share with the branch. There were two drive-up windows: one close to the building that a drawer extended out to grab whatever the customer would put in it and a satellite window where you would put your check, money, etc., in the tube and then place in the chute and press the button to send it through the chute to the building. This customer was at the satellite window. The teller, through the speaker, said yes, bring them in.

What no one could have predicted was he started putting them in the chute, one by one, and pressing send. They were not in the tube, so when they reached the place where the tube landed in the building, on impact, they got squashed and parts of the tomatoes flew out of the chute into various parts of the room. Some landed on the floor, some on the shelves, and some on the tellers, myself included. The teller at that drive-through window was trying to tell him she meant to bring the tomatoes in by walking into the branch, and he finally stopped. All of us in the branch, including customers, were hysterically laughing. It is one of those moments I will never forget and feel blessed that I was able to experience. The reactions of those trainers when they heard I was assigned Garden City now made perfect sense!

Halloween at the bank

When I worked at the branch, Thursday and Friday nights had lines outside the door. At that time there were seven tellers that lined up at the counter and drive-through, and now it's rare if you find two tellers in a branch. One typical Friday night, the line snaked around the lobby and went out the door. One of the tellers, Elaine, asked all of the tellers on the line if they had a roll of dimes she could buy. Another teller, Cheryl, said she did and instead of walking over to her to hand her the roll, Cheryl gently threw the roll of dimes to Elaine.

Elaine was sitting at her station; the throw was a little short so Elaine quickly reached out to catch the roll but forgot her cash drawer was open. She banged her chest into the drawer when she tried to catch the roll and yelled loudly, "Oh, my t- - !" The tellers and the lobby exploded with laughter, and Elaine was so embarrassed that she continued bending over to reach for the roll of coins and sat on the floor. The head teller came out of her office and took over Elaine's station to help customers. After the embarrassment decreased and the customers that were in line at the time she yelled were now replaced with new customers, Elaine did get off the floor and started taking care of customers again. This happened many years ago, but we still talk about the tomatoes and Elaine's incident when we see each other and we always laugh a lot.

When I transitioned into the audit department, everyone was nice, but I quickly realized that the environment was the opposite of the branch I just left. The bosses in the audit department were serious, stuffy, and conservative, which was the opposite of where I just left, and of my personality. I was the newest hire and some of the other auditors who also hadn't been there that long were very nice.

One day one of the auditors stopped in my cubicle and said come on, it's 10:30 a.m., break time. I followed him and watched what looked like a herd of auditors heading to the kitchen for a break. It was very strange to me that everyone went at the same time whether they wanted to or not. A couple of weeks in, the routine didn't change, and an auditor walked by my cubicle and told me it was break time. I replied, "I'll go in a few minutes." She came back to the entrance of my cubicle and asked what I meant. I said there are auditors that I don't want to sit with every day, so I am going later. About 20 minutes later I was heading to the kitchen with the herd heading toward me, and my boss, who I never liked, gave me a very disapproving, distinct look. Eventually, I did get some other auditors to change ranks and not go with the herd for a break. I knew this couldn't be helpful for my relationship with my boss.

As time went on and I traveled to many departments and many locations, I would hear, "You don't act like a typical auditor, you are not like them." I loved hearing that because I felt like I could get my job done and have some fun doing it. My boss didn't like hearing that. She was very controlling, and I always felt like she quickly realized it was a mistake hiring me.

I HAD HEARD THE BANK WAS CONNECTED WITH THE UNITED WAY. In August, the senior vice president of auditing called me into his office. He told me that every year the bank sends one employee for three months as a "Loaned Executive" to go work with an organization called United Way. The local chapter of United Way was based in Providence and its mission was to improve lives by mobilizing the caring power of communities around the world to advance the common good. He told me the selected employee would assist the organization in their fundraising campaign for various industries. The thought of getting out of the audit department for three months made me very happy. He then told me I was selected if I was willing to take the assignment. I gladly accepted and for the next three months, I worked for United Way.

*Last day working
for United Way*

There were about twenty-one categories of various industries at the United Way, and I was assigned health care. My job was to go to various hospitals and nursing homes and do presentations about United Way with the focus of getting as many donations as I could. The staff at United Way was incredible. Full of life and friendly, but very determined to help their organization. I worked with a supervisor, Jamie, who brought me to all the healthcare organizations in Rhode Island and introduced me to management.

Earlier that same year, the president of United Way, William Aramony, resigned over allegations of defrauding the organization of more than $1 million. He was convicted on twenty-three counts of felony charges, including conspiracy, fraud, and filing a false tax return, and spent six years in federal prison. I think every single one of the loaned executives had one person in their audience as they were presenting and asking for donations ask, "Why should I donate to an organization that the president will use to support his lavish lifestyle?" I had the same question in almost every healthcare facility I entered. It was not an easy environment to ask for donations because the scandal was all over the news just months before we started the fundraising campaign.

At the end of the three months, out of the twenty-one various categories, only five of them increased the amount of money brought in from the previous year. My area, health care, was one of them. I was so proud and grateful for my end results. On my last day at United Way, my supervisor Jamie took me out to lunch. I asked her if it was possible for me to apply for a position at United Way. I did not want to leave, and I especially did not want to go back to the bank.

Jamie brought me into her boss's office when we got back from lunch and I was saddened when her boss told me there was a clause in the loaned executive contract that prevented United Way from soliciting temporary workers or hiring them. He followed that up with saying that if that wasn't the case, he would absolutely have invited me to go through the interview process. That made me feel better, but didn't help the fact that I had to go back to the bank.

After a year-and-a-half of working for the audit department, I had several issues with my boss. I questioned her procedures several times and she did not like that. I knew she was trying any way she could to get me to leave her department. Finally, she called me into her office one morning and told me she was putting me on a thirty-day probationary period due to a multitude of things I did that went against audit policy. This was just a formality, and I knew at the end of the thirty days I would be "let go" from the bank. I couldn't let that happen; well, I wouldn't let it happen that way. She was not going to win.

In that thirty-day probation period, I was assigned a job with a small team at one of the branches that also housed an operations department. A couple of days prior to the thirty-day deadline, as I was working on this project, I pretended to fall when I was walking down some stairs heading to lunch with two other auditors. They were in front of me, so they never saw what happened. I had been planning this for several days. When they heard the noise, they turned around and helped me stand back up. They asked if I was okay, and I said yes. When we finished lunch and went back to the room we were based out of, one of the auditors told the lead auditor what had happened. She said she had to call in the incident to human resources even if I was okay. She did and then I spoke to a representative in human resources on the phone to explain what happened.

The next day I called in sick and told my boss I was very sore and my back was bothering me. A representative from human resources also called me the same day and told me I would need to go to their doctor to be evaluated. Several days later I did go see the doctor, who told me I would just need some therapy and I should be fine.

The day I was put on a thirty-day probation period, I began looking for a new job and sending out resumes. I had an interview with a company in Boston. I had been spending a lot of time in Massachusetts staying with Elix in his apartment, so Boston was a great location for a job. I did get an offer for a job, but was still waiting for the offer letter to come in the mail.

At this point, I had surpassed the thirty days by about six days, but I wasn't working so the probation period was extended. The following day I received the offer letter and was told my starting date. I smiled from ear to ear knowing what tomorrow would bring.

The following day, I went back to work at the bank with my resignation letter in my hand. I had a chance to chat with the auditors I liked, and they were very happy I was back. My boss was not an early person, so I had to wait for her to get to the office. I remember standing in my friend's cubicle, just talking, and seeing my boss's office light go on. Showtime! I walked into her office, placed my resignation letter on her desk in front of her, and said I am officially resigning today. She looked at the letter, then looked at me and said okay. The expression on her face was priceless. She didn't get to fire me, I left voluntarily, on my terms. I did say a couple of other things that I will omit here, but when I told Elix, my mom, and friends what I said to her, they all laughed hysterically. By the way, I won!

INSIGHT

Have fun. When you are feeling happy and loved, those same feelings come back to you. Every person is hit with hard times. When those times are occurring, you must be in touch and acknowledge the feelings you are experiencing. The key is to intentionally not to stay in that place for a significant period of time. Allow those feelings to run through your body, connect with them, and then start the process of moving away from them. When you are in a somber or even slight depression, it's extremely difficult to connect with spirit because they are on a completely different frequency.

CHAPTER 06

MOVING IN

I started my new job in Boston in November 1993. The commute was much easier staying with Elix in his apartment in Holbrook, Massachusetts as opposed to commuting from Providence.

Elix and I discussed the situation and we formally moved in together in December 1993, eight months after we met. He had a one-bedroom apartment with a kitchen, living room, and bathroom. I was also introduced to the love of his life, his cat Snowy. She was all white, with green eyes, and beautiful. I noticed immediately that Elix and Snowy had 100 percent trust and love for one another. It was quite remarkable. Snowy was very friendly and she accepted me almost overnight.

Having my first job in Boston was an amazing experience. Riding the train into the city was a first for me, and sometimes a bit overwhelming. I have had anxiety for as long as I remember, and it would kick in when I least expected it and sometimes last for weeks or for days. I never suspected that part of this anxiety had to do with spirit and energy waves running through my body at various times of the day. However, without any inclination that I was a Medium, I chalked the anxiety up to just who I was and that I needed to improve myself to get rid of the anxiety. Elix also worked in Boston and sometimes he needed to drive in to have his car with him to go to places during the day that weren't accessible by train. I loved it when he did that because I would drive with him and could avoid the train altogether.

I found myself again with such great people I was working with. The company was called First Data and dealt with mutual funds. The office was across the street from the iconic Faneuil Hall Marketplace in Boston, so my friends and I would go to lunch there often or just hang out and watch people.

I was quickly promoted to manager of this relatively new department called quality assurance. I had about ten individuals working for me. I moved into a new office, still a cubicle, but now it was a corner office overlooking Faneuil Hall. I loved it because the windows went from the ceiling to the floor, so my office was filled with light all the time. There was a plant in my new cubicle, so I adopted it and took care of it. That was in 1994 and I have that plant sitting in my home right now.

About two-and-a-half years in, we were told that our department would be moving out of Boston and into Westboro, a city about forty-five minutes from Boston. None of us were happy about the move. Luckily, the company provided a temporary shuttle from Boston to Westboro, so about 90 percent of my staff transferred to Westboro. The shuttle would be in place for three months and then the employees would have to arrange their own transportation if they continued working in Westboro. Many of the staff carpooled to Westboro, including myself. The Westboro location was enormous, but the Boston location would always have a special place in my heart.

After we settled in Westboro, I received some more news that my boss Dan would be temporarily working in another location, north of Boston. I was devastated because we got along so well and because something told me he wasn't coming back to my department, and he never did. My department was unique because all the other departments were categorized as operations, but my department was categorized as audit. A couple of months later, I was notified that Dan wasn't coming back to my department so they would temporarily have me reporting to the Senior Vice President, Gerry. This was about a three-or-four-level jump, and I was thrown into meetings with all high-level executives.

I remember walking over to Gerry's office and asking his assistant if he was there. He wasn't, but she called me over to show me something on her computer. I walked around her desk and stood next to her, and I remember her saying "I want to show you something called the World Wide Web." I had no idea that this would be my first exposure to the internet. She showed me how it worked, and I thought it was so cool. She was such a nice lady and she always took care of me in any way she could.

One morning Gerry called me and asked me to come into his office. When I got there, he told me he was not available enough for me to have him as his direct report. He told me I would be reporting to Julie, the Director of Operations. I told him immediately that is not appropriate as my department evaluates all the operational departments and scores them weekly. This would be a big conflict. He reassured me that this was just temporary, and that they are interviewing for the position that I would report to. I saw the writing on the wall that this was not going to be an easy ride.

Almost immediately, I clashed with Julie. Besides the obvious stated above, she was bossy, cranky, and a micromanager. I had never had a boss like that since I started working for the company. One late afternoon, I was sitting at the desk of one of my staff members, Rosie, and we were just chatting. Julie walked over to me, said she was leaving, and also said, "I know you don't like me, I can see it in your eyes." She then just stared at me waiting for a response like, "That's not true." For about five seconds, I just stared back saying nothing. She turned around and stormed out and Rosie had the pleasure of telling the entire staff about that incident. None of my staff liked Julie so they loved hearing the story.

INSIGHT

My maternal grandfather Fred, who was deceased before I was born, told his four daughters that you teach people how to treat you and don't take any sh- - from people. I don't believe you can trust anyone or anything unless you trust yourself first. When you trust yourself, you put yourself first which makes you not afraid of standing up for yourself. The foundation for connecting with spirit is trust. I have never worried about the potential outcomes of standing up for what I believe because I know it would always work out to my advantage.

CHAPTER 07

LAW SCHOOL

In 1995, I started applying to Law School. I took the LSAT and obtained a great score. My mother loved to tell me the story of her going to see a psychic named Ellie when we were young. She told my mom that one of her boys would be an attorney. At that point, I was probably about nine or ten years old. My mom didn't see her again, but I always loved hearing that story. I remember trying to process how Ellie received that information and how I would love to be able to do that.

I applied to a couple of law schools, and I was accepted to Southern New England School of Law, which is now University of Massachusetts Law School in North Dartmouth, Massachusetts. I applied to be in the part-time program, which held classes on Tuesday and Thursday evenings and Saturday days. I knew I would still be working full time so the part-time program would work best for me. Elix was so supportive and so happy I was accepted.

The first year, there were three courses you would take: Property, Torts, and Contracts. They were full-year courses so we started in August and you received your final grade in May of the following year. In May of 1997, I received my grades. I passed Contracts with 70 percent and the other two grades were both below 60 percent. I was devastated,embarrassed, and knew my law school dream was over. I cried the entire car ride home and the hardest thing was to tell this news to Elix. After I told him, he hugged me and consoled me to the best of his ability. I was not an easy person to deal with when I was in this kind of mood.

Several weeks later, Elix talked to me about reaching out to the school and seeing if I could return and take the first year over again. I said, "Are you crazy?" On my first day of classes, one of the professors told the students "Look to the left and look to the right, at least one of the students you just looked at won't be here next year." I was adamant about not reaching out to the school, but after another week- I am not sure what happened- but I changed my mind (all due to Elix).

I made an appointment with my Torts professor and explained to her that I was prepared for those exams and that I knew the answers to the essays. She told me I could appeal the automatic dismissal due to my grades, but warned it was extremely rare to get the school to reverse their decision. I went forward and appealed the school's decision. The school's committee reviewed my exams with the applicable professors of the respective classes: it took about three weeks and then I got a phone call. One of the committee members told me after evaluating my exams, they were reversing the dismissal and allowing me to come back to the program, but I needed to retake the entire first year. The same day, my Torts professor also called me and said the committee had never seen responses to exams like mine, it was a first. Clearly, I was very prepared and knowledgeable, but the answers were all over the place with no flow or consistency. I was so excited but also so apprehensive because all the students in my class would know I had to repeat the first year.

After long discussions with Elix, I decided to return. However, I decided to only take Property and Torts because I did pass Contracts with a 70 percent. At the end of my second year, my grades were 96 percent and 94 percent and I proceeded to my second year (well, third year) of law school.

In my last year of law school, I was called into the Dean's office. The Dean had left the school for another position and the Assistant Dean was temporarily in the Dean role. He brought me in because it came to his attention that I never repeated Contracts. I told him I passed Contracts on the first try so I didn't think I needed to take the class again. He responded with the requirements for you to come back were to take all three first-year courses. Of course, I knew that was the requirement but decided not to retake the class. He looked at my transcript and said, "It looks like you do whatever you want without regard to procedures." He said this would have to be brought up by the committee and they would vote on whether I needed to repeat Contracts before graduating. Thankfully, the committee voted to waive re-taking contracts and I am sure it was because my grades were all A's.

I graduated from Law School in June of 2001 and immediately started studying for the Bar examination, which was given in July.

Law School Graduation

Elix and I booked a room at the Seaport Hotel in Boston, right across from the building where the bar exam was administered. The Bar exam was a two-day exam. The first day consisted of one hundred multiple-choice questions in the morning, 9 a.m. to 12 p.m., and one hundred in the afternoon, 1 p.m. to 4 p.m. The second day was five essay questions in the morning and five in the afternoon. At the end of the first day, I met Elix back in the room crying because the exam was so hard and I felt that I didn't do well on the multiple-choice questions. I was never so happy for the second day to end but also felt the same way; this exam was brutally hard. Previously, an attorney told me, "If you think the exam wasn't that bad when you finished taking it, you did not pass the exam." But the worst part was waiting three months to get the results by mail.

September 11, 2001, Elix was working for Easter Seals and he left early in the morning. I wasn't working that day and I ran out to Dunkin Donuts to get coffee. I came back into the house, put the TV on, and I thought I was seeing things. A plane crashed into one of the Twin Towers and the announcer I was listening to was in disbelief. I was staring at the TV when I saw the second plane come and crash into the other tower. Most people can remember exactly where they were when this happened. It clearly changed the world and would negatively affect the economy for months.

At that time, Elix was part-time coaching for an organization and would go to New York City where the training and sessions were held at the World Trade Centers. I also went with him a couple of times. We must have had help from above to make sure Elix wasn't there that day. My brother, sister-in-law, and nephew lived in New York City at the time, and ironically my nephew's birthday is on September 11, just a different year.

One November day, I got word that the Bar exam results were mailed out. That day and for the next two, I stood at the bay window waiting for the mailman to walk up to our front door and deliver our mail. I told Elix I would wait for him to get home on the day I received the results, but I would call him to let him know I received them. Late one morning, I saw the mailman heading towards my house. As soon as he left the porch, I opened the door and grabbed the mail. I saw the envelope from the State of Massachusetts and I knew it was the results. I could also see a green paper inside so I immediately thought I didn't pass, and that green paper was the information on the next Bar exam which would be in February (the Bar exam is given twice a year). I called Elix and told him I had the envelope.

We both agreed for me to change the plans and open the envelope while he was on the phone. I did and the first thing I saw at the top of the page was "We are pleased to inform you..." I passed the exam!!!! I screamed on the phone, Elix screamed in his office and I heard cheers in the background where Elix was. It was the best feeling. I called my mother next to tell her the good news. That night we drove to Providence and the three of us went out to dinner at Julio's in North Providence to celebrate. There were a lot of tears of joy that night.

I was sworn in as a Massachusetts attorney in January 2002. The ceremony was in Boston and it was an experience I will never forget. The great thing was I was now an attorney, the bad thing was, jobs were almost impossible to obtain due to September 11th and its aftermath.

PERSONAL INJURY was not something I was interested in. I briefly worked for a small personal injury law firm, but the commute was long and I didn't enjoy working on personal injury cases. In my last year of law school, I took a class called Juvenile Law. I fell in love with it and studied for the final exam for about one hour and got a 97 percent on the final exam. I remember my Juvenile Law professor telling me about a wonderful opportunity to work for the state as a contractor in Juvenile Court. I investigated that lead and needed to complete an application to be selected to take the course and become certified. Once certified, your name was added to a list and that list was used to assign clients to attorneys. The certifications only happened twice a year and it was very hard to get accepted, even with years of legal experience.

My thought was to get some experience quickly so I could include that in my application. I researched and found that there were volunteers that were necessary for foster care reviews for children in foster care. I didn't know exactly what the role was, but I applied and was accepted very quickly as a volunteer. My role was to be part of a three-person independent panel for foster children to ensure the state was providing these kids with what they needed. I really enjoyed being part of this panel. I had one meeting and that information went on my application to be certified to represent children.

It was about one month later, and I received a letter saying I was accepted into the certification program. Once I started representing children in Juvenile Court, I couldn't count how many attorneys would come up to me and ask how I got accepted right out of law school. I would say luck, but I knew there was another driving force: spirit.

After becoming certified, I started representing children and parents in Brockton Juvenile Court. You were allowed to work in Juvenile Court in two counties, so to add income I also worked in New Bedford Juvenile Court. As time went on, I was very busy representing children and parents in both courts. I wasn't too thrilled about representing parents, but that was part of the certification and as cases came into court, the clerk would go down the list and appoint attorneys in order of the list. You had the same probability of representing children as you did parents.

After about three years of working in Juvenile Court, I was assigned to represent a mother on a care & protection case, with allegations that she was abusing her children. I met with her in the conference room to prepare for the trial, and I realized quickly that she knew the system very well. She told me some things that she knew as her attorney I needed to keep confidential, and by just hearing some of these things, my opinion was she should not have custody of her children.

That evening I came home completely exhausted, crying, and asking Elix how was I supposed to do my best to represent this mother with the goal of getting her children back to her after knowing what she said to me? I knew I couldn't continue in this capacity unless I could only represent children. Unfortunately that wasn't an option, so I decided to take a break from Juvenile Court. But now what would I do?

In the interim, I figured I could rely on my accounting degree, so I applied for an accountant's position at a property management company and surprisingly I got the job. I worked there for a year and-a-half and about halfway through my tenure, I told the accounting manager that I was an attorney. He was surprised but very impressed. Once the cat was out of the bag, I completed a proposal that I presented to the owner of the company to use me as in-house counsel for evictions, etc., instead of an outside firm. He liked the proposal and my initiative, but wasn't interested in changing anything, so I decided to start looking for another job.

I landed a job as the assistant director for a housing project that would utilize my property management skills as well as my legal skills. The woman acting as the temporary director would stay until I was up to speed to step into that position. From the first moment I met her, I didn't like her. She was very demeaning to all the office staff, and nobody liked her. One afternoon she told me I needed to tell the staff that if a resident had more than one dog (two was the maximum), they needed to pay two seventy-five dollar fees on an annual basis as opposed to one. That night I looked up the federal laws and statutes and found the maximum fee to charge residents regardless of whether they had one or two dogs was seventy-five dollars. I knew that when I addressed this with the director in the morning, it would not go well.

The next morning, the director walked into my office and sat down to discuss some issues. I told her what I found in the Federal laws about the maximum amount to charge residents for pet fees and she told me I was wrong, and that they needed to be charged two fees. I told her I was not wrong, she was wrong, and I was not charging two fees when the law says there is a maximum of one fee. We went back and forth with this same subject a couple of times and then it broadened out to other issues. After about fifteen minutes, she jumped out of her seat, crying, and briskly walked to her office, which was on the other side of the building. One of the staff members came into my office right after the director left and said, "What happened, she was crying?" Before I could explain what happened, the staff member hugged me and said thank you, it was about time she was the one crying and not the rest of us.

I started packing up my office and grabbing anything I thought I needed from it because I knew what was coming. About thirty minutes later, from my window I saw the Chair of the Board driving up and coming into the building. The director's assistant called me and said the director wanted to see me in her office. I walked in with the director and they asked me to take a seat. They handed me a document and said I was being terminated, effective immediately for insubordination. One big relief was I never would have to see that director's face ever again, but the sad part was never seeing the staff again, or at least not seeing them on a daily basis.

I found out a couple of days later that at the following open management meeting, many residents, after hearing I was fired, showed up at the meeting demanding they hire me back. I loved meeting those residents. I still have beautiful cards that some of the residents wrote me after my termination. I never realized I could make an impact on so many residents after only three months. It warms my heart every time I think of those wonderful people.

Next I briefly worked for a company based out of Virginia. Various companies would offer their employees legal representation if they ever needed an attorney, and it was a fee that would come out of their paychecks. My position was an attorney that took the calls from employees that had legal questions or needed legal representation. I would answer the questions and do a referral to attorneys in their area for representation. This position was nice because you worked from home but never interacted with anyone in person and just being connected to a headset was not for me. I have always loved interacting with people in person so this remote job was hard for me to continue.

STARTING MY OWN BUSINESS was something I had been thinking about for a while. In 2008, I decided to take the plunge and start my own business in Probate Court. Elix had been in health care for a number of years and had many executive contacts in hospitals and nursing homes. I knew most of the healthcare facilities used outside counsel for their guardianships and conservatorship needs. I also knew that the two main companies had a hold on most of the healthcare facilities, but that wasn't going to stop me. With Elix's help, I scheduled meetings with the presidents or high-level management and proposed doing their guardianships and conservatorships for less than what they were currently paying other attorneys. Some facilities had no interest in changing whom they were using but some said they would give me a shot to see what I could do. The ones that gave me an opportunity, I scrambled to do whatever I could to get these things done for them. My contacts in the healthcare facilities were always social workers, so I was extremely nice to all of them. Social workers are also notorious for jumping to several different organizations and once they have moved to another facility, they worked their magic to get me working there also. After a couple of years, I was working in Probate Court in most counties in Massachusetts. Ironically, at the same time, I received an email from the state notifying me they now had attorneys who only represent children for CRA's (Children Requiring Assistance) and asked if I would be interested in coming back to Juvenile Court. I said yes immediately and went back in 2009 to representing children, but for less serious issues, i.e., skipping school, running away, misbehaving at home, etc. These listed issues are of course serious, but to a lesser degree compared to abuse and neglect cases.

INSIGHT

When I look back at my life, I realize there had to be more than just luck accompanying me. The fact that my law school reversed their decision and allowed me back in was remarkable, but also getting a one-year course waived a month before graduation was astounding. I've always known I had help from spirit, but I had no idea the extent of this help. To connect with spirit, you don't need to know what is going on backstage. It may feel like it has been a long time since you felt your loved ones in spirit or saw a sign from them. There is so much occurring behind the scenes and the people that enhance their skills in connecting to spirit are the ones that know spirit is with them, and it's just a matter of time before there is constant connection.

CHAPTER 08

SPIRIT MAKES ITS MOVE

I have always loved Halloween. I am not sure what I would have done if Elix didn't also love Halloween, but I don't have to worry about that because he loves it too. He was also born in October and thinks he's more connected with the holiday due to that fact. We are also fortunate to live in Massachusetts, where Salem is located: the most iconic witch city in the world! Every year, since I became an adult, I have gone to Salem in October for Halloween events. There is something about this city that makes me feel at home. Knowing the history and the connection with witches from centuries ago gets my energy charged. I always feel very magical there and love getting a reading from one of the psychics.

The stores have a unique smell as you walk in, a smell I never experience other than in Salem. The candles, the incense, crystals, witch balls, etc.; I always want to take one of each home.

We always go to Salem on the closest weekend to Halloween. If Halloween fell on a Saturday or Sunday, we would all dress in costumes during our visit. That weekend was like a giant Halloween party with people in costumes wherever you looked, inside or outside.

One year when we went to Salem for Halloween, we signed up for a psychic reading at Crow Haven. Crow Haven is the oldest witch shop in Salem and the owner is Lorelei, a witch, psychic, and Medium, and a wonderful human being. As luck would have it, Elix and I asked to go for the reading together and we got assigned to Lorelei. After that reading, Elix and I became friends with Lorelei and we see her at least once a year when we travel to Salem.

Ever since my first visit, when I'm walking around Salem I feel like I am home. I can't quite explain the feeling, but I feel like I fit in with the witches and other magical people there. It's a tradition that every time I go to Salem, I buy some type of witch. It can be big or small, and several years ago I purchased a little witch with a string attached that hangs off my rear- view mirror no matter which car I have. Seeing her riding her broom and swinging back and forth always brings a smile to my face.

For a while, Elix and I were big into herbs and crystals. We would tell Lorelei what we wanted to focus on, such as protection, love, or money, and she would select various herbs or crystals and put them in a velvet pouch. At one point, I had three pouches that were somewhere located in my Burberry bag that I would bring to court. It always made me feel good that they were there.

I WAS ANXIOUS TO SEE A MEDIUM, so in February 2010, I purchased two tickets for Elix and myself to go and see a local Medium. It was a great venue with about ninety people in the audience. Elix and I were in the front row and all day long I begged my father to come through and let me know he was with me. I was very anxious heading to the venue and even more anxious sitting in the room waiting for the Medium to come out and start reading people.

She was right on time. She came out, introduced herself, and explained how the night would go, but I heard nothing she said because I was still having a conversation with my dad and telling him he had to come through. The Medium was ready to start, looked over the room, and started walking towards me. I was hoping she was coming to me, but at the same time I was very nervous. She walked up to me, stood in front of me, and asked me my name. I said it was Steven, but I remembered from her introduction that she said if I come up to you, I will ask you to stand. She was just staring at me but wasn't asking me to stand up. After about fifteen seconds, she looked at me and said, "You are a psychic but don't know it." I heard what sounded like some gasps in the audience and in the blink of an eye, it was over. She moved on to the second person and asked them to stand up and read them for several minutes.

Minutes after she left me, Elix tapped me and said, "Did you hear what she said?" I thought I did, but asked Elix to repeat it. He said, "She said you are a psychic and don't know it." I looked at Elix and said she was crazy because I am not a psychic. During her presentation, she walked by me and told me my grandmother was standing next to me but then just kept walking to the next person she was reading. Her event went on for about two hours and Elix said when she finished that I should ask her what she meant when she came up to me. I agreed, but at the end of the night there were

SPIRIT MAKES ITS MOVE

many people chatting with her and waiting to speak to her, so I got frustrated and said to Elix let's go. However, I couldn't stop thinking about what she said to me.

The next morning, I went on her website and looked up her email address. I sent her a message explaining who I was and what had transpired the night before. To my surprise, she answered me within fifteen minutes (I still have a copy of that email). She said she wanted to thank me because she was very tired last night, and she felt like my energy helped her to connect with spirit. I had no idea what she was talking about. She did want to talk to me at the end of the night and looked for us, but we were gone. She ultimately offered for me to go to her workshop that was coming up and sold out, but Elix and I had planned that particular weekend to go to New York City so I told her I wasn't available. We didn't get into any more specifics about what she told me, I just knew I couldn't shake the feeling.

Over the next two years, nothing out of the ordinary happened. During the summer of 2012, I started experiencing more anxiety than I ever had before. I had episodes of what felt like waves of energy surging through my body and as time went on, the episodes started occurring more frequently. There were times I felt like I wanted to jump out of my body because the unfamiliar feeling was penetrating my entire body. It always seemed to increase when I was in the car. In hindsight, I don't think it was the car itself. I think I was feeling the energy of loved ones trying to communicate with the people I was traveling to see.

In September 2012 I was browsing through Petfinder, an internet site where you can adopt rescue dogs. We already had two Japanese Chins who were both rescues, Rico and Little Ricky. I happened to see a Japanese Chin puppy named Memphis, and I fell in love with him. He was found down South, like many of them are, and rescued and brought to the North for adoption. I copied the picture of Memphis and sent it to Elix to see if he was open to a third dog coming into the family. He fell in love with him as soon as he saw his picture. I almost immediately filled out the application and sent it off, hoping Memphis was not already adopted.

Within hours, we found out Memphis was ours. The foster mom said Albany, New York would be the halfway mark for us to meet and pick up Memphis. We picked a day to meet her and meet Memphis. On the drive to Albany, we took Rico and Little Ricky. Both were in their carry-on bags with seatbelts in the back seat. We pulled into a parking lot and saw a woman getting out of a van holding this black-and-white furball. Memphis was beautiful. Neither one of us wanted to stop hugging him, but we put him down and introduced him to Rico and Little Ricky. They all seemed to get along. Rico and Little Ricky were never barkers. Occasionally when someone rang the doorbell you would hear one or both bark, but that was about it. We quickly realized that wasn't going to be the case with Memphis.

The entire two-and-a-half hours home, Memphis was barking, crying, or whining. The other two dogs were sleeping, but Memphis let us know he was in the back seat. Memphis was potty trained very quickly and fell into a routine fast also. We suspected Memphis had been abused or neglected prior to him coming to us. The five of us would be laying on the bed at night and watching TV and Memphis, in deep sleep, would start this high- pitched crying like someone was stabbing him, and once he opened his eyes and realized where he was, the screaming stopped. We would immediately hold him and comfort him and eventually, after several weeks, the crying stopped permanently.

At this time, I had my probate business in full swing. My office was in the house so when I wasn't in court, I was in the home office. Memphis was still very loud with his barking all day. I was dealing with my increased anxiety and having Memphis around constantly barking was not helping me deal with this horrible feeling. Elix was still working in the healthcare industry, so he left every day for work and didn't come back until mid-to- late afternoon.

Elix saw how I was being affected by Memphis. At that time, anything that was out of the ordinary would drive me crazy. I told Elix I didn't know if I could handle keeping Memphis, so he devised a plan. To help me, Elix would take Memphis to work with him as much as he could. He never asked anyone at the office whether he could bring Memphis, he just did. That helped me so much in trying to deal with my anxiety. During this time, Elix and Memphis created a bond between the two of them that I know will never happen with Elix and another animal again.

After things settled down, Elix would always say he would have done anything he needed to do to make sure Memphis stayed in our family. He knew if we ever gave him away, at some point the realization of not having him, due to me, would have scarred me for life. That is no exaggeration. I love Elix for many reasons, but this one is very special to me. Our boy, Memphis, crossed the rainbow bridge in October 2020 at only nine years old. This was the toughest thing Elix had ever gone through and he is still processing it. Elix's heart will never be the same and just this week Elix said to me, "Eventually when I die, I know Memphis will be the first dog or person I will see." Memphis gives Elix signs all the time that he is around. Just a couple of days ago I had a visit from him, not a dream but a visit, which I have not stopped smiling and thinking about.

TAKING MEDIUM CLASSES was not something I had thought about. Elix surprised me with one of my Christmas presents in 2012; he bought me a sixteen-week home-study course to become a certified Medium. I was very excited and curious about this course. It was created by Carol Nicholson who is one of, if not the most, incredibly talented psychics I have ever met and so much more. When the class was live,

Carol recorded all the phone sessions (this was before Zoom was popular) with the students so I had the audio and the written materials that accompanied the audio. Once I started the first chapter, I could not put that course down. Every spare second I had I was listening and reading.

I emailed Carol when I first got to her course to let her know I was very impressed and was starting with the first chapter. When I finished the course, there was a final test that I needed to complete. What surprised me was after I completed the test, I needed to send it to Carol and set up a final interview with her. I reached out to Carol, told her I was finished with the course, completed the test, and emailed it to her. This was about four weeks after I started the course. She was shocked and said she had never seen anyone go through the course so quickly and complete the test that fast. We set up the phone call; I had no idea what this would be like, and I was very nervous.

I called Carol on the date and time we scheduled my phone call. It was so nice to hear her voice and she started going through the test questions and my answers. After the review, she said, "The only thing left is for you to do a reading for me." This took me by complete surprise. A reading, now, on the phone, is she nuts? But she was so great and guided me through it. She said to start with a remote reading, which means you tune into where she is and start picking up items near her, the color of the walls in the room, where she is sitting, items in the room, etc.

I did my best to tune in, and I brought up a lamp I could see in my third eye. I described it and she told me I had just described the lamp she was sitting next to. Then I did straight Mediumship and brought through her mother and grandmother, and based on Carol's responses, there were several validations. I then was done with the call and Carol sent me a decree stating I finished the sixteen-week course to be a certified Medium. I was so excited but then I thought, **how do I use this?**

Carol and I became friends and she still is a mentor to me. Any time I have a question I email her, and she never fails to respond with answers that help me so much. My goal is to one day meet her in person; she lives in Arizona, and I know that will happen. In my office in New Bedford, I have about five framed decrees hanging on my wall from various classes I have taken with Carol. I did most of them live via the phone which was amazing.

INSIGHT

It is very easy to put limits on ourselves. Over the years, I have heard people say, "I'm not smart enough," "I'm too old," "I don't have enough money," and "That only happens to those kinds of people." If I didn't remove my limits, I would have never gone to law school. It would have been so easy to use limits like, I am not smart enough or going part-time and working would be too much work, etc. Connecting to spirit needs a limitless thought process. It's easy to limit what you believe about spirit because you can't physically see it. Those are limits. Start small by expanding your limits and once you see the results, your goal will be to remove all limits!

CHAPTER 09

AM I GOING CRAZY?

We had been living in our new house for eight years. We had a doorbell that was installed when we first moved in that gave you the option of playing six different songs when someone rang the bell. About seven years ago, there was a malfunction in the doorbell so when somebody rang the bell you would hear this computerized voice say, "Install Cover." We pulled that cover off the base of the doorbell and put it back on again more times than we could count, and it never fixed the doorbell. We never had an urgency to fix it and were okay with "Install Cover."

On June 14, 2013, my birthday, we were having a small gathering for dinner at our house. We were, and still are, very friendly with our then neighbors, John and Darlene. They are the best people! They were invited to the dinner but already had plans so they couldn't make it. They did say they would briefly stop by on their way out to say happy birthday. It was about 4 p.m. and the doorbell rang and to my surprise, it wasn't "Install Cover." Instead, it was playing the birthday song. I was upstairs when the doorbell rang, and I couldn't wait to go downstairs to thank Elix for doing that for me. On the way down the staircase, I was thinking when did Elix do that?

Elix was just about to open the front door and let John and Darlene in when I yelled out, "Elix, I love the birthday song, and thank you for doing that." With one hand on the doorknob, he turned and looked at me and said, "I didn't touch that doorbell." John and Darlene came in and one of them commented on the birthday song. Elix and I looked at each other in confusion. How did that happen? For the rest of the evening, every time the doorbell rang (which was just a couple more times) the birthday song played. At the end of the night, I asked Elix if he thought the birthday song would still play tomorrow. He said he assumed it would, but we would find out tomorrow.

The next morning, Elix followed me out of the bedroom and stood at the top of the staircase watching me head to the front door. I opened the door, reached outside, and pressed the doorbell. What did we hear but "Install Cover." It reverted to what it had been playing for the last seven years. The two of us could not believe this and we were very perplexed. I said to Elix that it must be spirit.

It was July 2012, and I received a phone call from my cousin, Holly, that her father had passed away. Her mom and my mom were sisters and her mom, my aunt, had already passed away. My cousin and family lived in Florida, but the service was going to be held at my best friend Paul's funeral home in East Providence, Rhode Island. I knew he would do an amazing job with the service.

Everything was held in the funeral home. There were not a lot of people at the wake, mostly family and friends of the family. I was at the doorway of the room where my uncle was laid out in his coffin. There were two people sitting in chairs at the side of the room but no one else. I was staring at the coffin and my uncle and started to think about his wife, my aunt. I remember thinking, Auntie, I know you were there when Uncle passed away and I know you are at the coffin right now. At the precise second I had that thought, I saw the crucifix that was attached to the lid of the coffin, which was open, fall into the coffin.

Paul walked up to me at the same time to ask me how I was doing. I told him I was just staring at the coffin and the crucifix fell into the coffin. He looked at the coffin and said, "Did someone grab it?" I said no, no one was near the coffin. He said that was impossible because the crucifix was securely attached to the lid of the coffin. We both walked over to the coffin and Paul saw the cross lying on my uncle's chest. He said the metal holder was still securely in place and he didn't understand how the cross fell with the holder still in place. There was no doubt in my mind that it was spirit.

August 25 has always been a special day for me because it was the day that my father took his life. In 2012 we were thinking about selling the house I grew up in because it needed so much work in so many areas of the house;being a three-story house, that was a lot of work. I was going through some boxes in the basement, and I found my paternal grandmother Rose's birth certificate. I had never seen that before and never met any of my grandparents as they had all crossed over before I was born. Unfortunately for me, it was in Polish which meant I couldn't read it. I was so excited to find this and immediately looked for her birth date because I never knew it. It read **25 Sierpien**. I assumed it was September 25, but I wanted to make sure I was right.

I took the birth certificate with me to my dentist's office about one month after finding it because I had a cleaning scheduled. I remembered that one of the dentist's assistants was from Poland and spoke fluent Polish. Before I left the dentist's office, I asked to see her. I gave her the birth certificate and asked if she could tell me what my grandmother's birthday is. She looked at it and said, "She was born on August 25." I said that I thought it was September based on the closeness to the English spelling, but she said it's definitely August. I thanked her and walked out of the dentist's office feeling so happy I finally knew my grandmother's birthday.

On the drive home, the thought randomly popped into my head, **Oh, my god, my father killed himself on his mother's birthday!** My mom used to tell me how close he was to his mother. All these years, how could I have never known that? Clearly, my mom didn't know or remember her mother- in-law's birthday because she would have told me. I couldn't wait to see Elix and tell him what I found out. It took me several days to process the fact that my dad chose his mom's birthday to take his life.

After learning the above-stated information, one thing I started noticing about two or three weeks before August 25 I would get signs from both my dad and my grandmother. After a couple of years, I started expecting the signs, and it turned into almost like a ritual.

BIRTHDAYS OR ANNIVERSARIES ALWAYS SEEMED TO BRING SIGNS.On August 25, 2012, Elix, myself, and another best friend, Susan, went to "Onset Illumination Bay." It is a festival held in the town of Onset where the perimeter of the bay is lit up with lanterns at dusk. I had heard about this event but none of us had ever gone. It also was my father's anniversary of death and my grandmother's (his mom's) birthday. The three of us went to dinner prior to the event and Susan asked me if I had received any signs from my dad since it was his anniversary. I replied not as of yet, but you never know.

After dinner, the three of us found a bench to sit on because dusk was about thirty minutes away. I was talking to Susan when Elix said, "Who the hell do you have as your profile picture on Facebook?" I looked at him and said, "Me, why?" He said that is not a picture of you. I grabbed my phone and looked at Facebook and my profile was a picture of a guy that I did not recognize. I said, "How is this possible?" I asked Susan to check her Facebook and when she did she said I see a guy's picture on your profile that is not you. Elix then realized he knew this guy but also said he lives in Israel. I then realized, this is my dad doing this. My dad was the ultimate jokester and loved making people laugh. I told Elix and Susan, this is my dad, and I thanked him for giving me such a wild sign. Susan said it was unbelievable.

At some point on the drive home, I looked back at Facebook and my profile was back to a picture of me. That night, before bed, I acknowledged him and thanked him for sending me the sign and for reminding me he is always with me.

On August 25, 2013, Elix, his mom, and I were heading to Faneuil Hall in Boston to walk around and have dinner. I reminded Elix that today wasn't just the anniversary of my father's death but also my grandmother Rose's birthday. I also told him I just know she will give me some kind of sign today to let me know she is with me. After walking around and doing some shopping, we selected a restaurant to go to and eat. We were sitting at the table and I thought, ***Maybe our server, if a woman, will be named Rose.*** It was a woman, but she introduced herself as Lauren. At that point, I started questioning whether I was just nuts and if I would get a sign from my grandmother Rose.

Toward the end of the meal, Elix asked our server how long she had worked for the restaurant. She responded with, "Only three months, I worked for the past two years at another restaurant called the Black Rose." I almost jumped out of my chair with excitement. Grandma Rose gave me a sign on her birthday, and it made me feel amazing.

INSIGHT

Our loved ones in spirit send signs to us daily. One person does not get more signs than another person daily. Our loved ones in spirit also select which kind of signs they want to send us. The top ten signs that spirit sends us are:

01. *Coins*
02. *Vivid Dreams (a visit not a dream)*
03. *Feathers*
04. *Anything with wings: birds, butterflies, dragonflies, etc.*
05. *Orbs in pictures/movies*
06. *Shadows out of the corner of your eye*
07. *Smelling a fragrance*
08. *Specific numbers appearing*
09. *Flickering/blowing out light bulbs*

Remember: Spirit sending signs is the easy part. The recipient seeing the signs is the challenging part.

CHAPTER 10

WAS THAT A PREMONITION?

D uring the winter of 2011, Elix found out that his dad was diagnosed with multiple myeloma. Multiple myeloma is cancer that accumulates in the bone marrow and crowds out healthy blood cells. It can cause severe bone pain and other symptoms. There are no cures but there are many treatments for the diagnosis.

When I first met Servo, Elix's father, he barely spoke English but was very nice to me. Elix's parents have a large backyard and that is where Servo would spend most of his day. He had chickens and roosters and would be out there taking care of them for hours. He also had several dogs that stayed in the backyard and one, Negrito, who was tiny and black, stayed in the house. Servo loved animals and reminded me of a story my mom would tell me about her father, my grandfather. My grandfather Fred loved animals. One day a Medium-sized black dog got hit by a car and broke his back legs. My grandfather then made splints for both his back legs until his legs healed. He named him Blackie. My mom used to say that when my grandfather took the splints off, Blackie walked like a seal. I never understood what that meant but I guess he didn't walk like a normal dog. My grandfather also told his daughters, "If you don't like animals, you are not a good person." That is one of two mottos I live by.

Due to Servo's diagnosis, Elix and I started going to Puerto Rico, where his dad still lived, for shorter time periods but more frequently. Elix made a point to be in Puerto Rico for his father's doctors' appointments and his father appreciated that. Due to the pain Elix's father was experiencing, he was taking various medications. Some of the medications caused his dad to retain water and much of his body became swollen. It was tough to see his dad in that condition and his memory was also being affected. Elix's mom was taking care of him in their house.

Elix's relationship with his dad was rocky at times. In June 2012, we went to Puerto Rico for several days. Elix's dad had deteriorated a little since we last saw him, but he was still mobile and living at home. We were staying at the Ponce Hilton which was about five minutes from Elix's parents' house. The night before we left to come back home to Massachusetts, we were in bed and turned off the lights to go to bed. I closed my eyes and something very strange happened. I saw a vision. It was like watching a mini movie clip that was blurry and moving very fast. I saw a man standing and grabbing the back of his neck with one hand and sort of swaying. Then he fell to the ground and the movie disappeared. I knew it was a man, but I had no idea who the man was. The feeling that accompanied the movie was someone having a heart attack, but this was a guess on my part. The entire movie happened in about three seconds, and it was something I had never experienced. As I layed in bed, I thought, **What do I do with this information? Was this a premonition? Would this come true? Would it be soon?** I was overwhelmed with thoughts about what had just happened and how I would handle the vision.

The first person I thought about was Elix's dad. It was natural for him to pop into my head because of his diagnosis and his health status. However, if this was a heart attack it didn't make sense that this could be Servo because he didn't have any issues with his heart. After thinking about this for thirty minutes, I grabbed my cell phone from the table next to me and thought it would be a great idea to email myself a description of what happened. If I did that, I wouldn't forget about it and maybe I could figure out why I saw this vision.

I thought about telling Elix, who was lying next to me, but considering what was going on with his dad, I decided not to bring it up. The next morning, we stopped at Elix's parent's house before we headed to the airport. Elix told his dad that he loved him, and they were both crying. In almost twenty years of being with Elix, I had never seen this level of emotion or connection between Elix and his dad. It was very moving. Elix knew that that would be the last time he would see his dad alive. Elix mentioned to me that he wasn't sure how he knew it would be the last time, he just knew. Elix is also very connected to spirit. I have loved watching how he has strengthened that connection over the years.

We were not home for more than twenty-four hours when Elix got a call from his niece that his dad had passed away. We hadn't put the suitcases away and immediately started packing them again to head back to Puerto Rico. We took the 1 a.m. flight from Boston to Puerto Rico and arrived at 4:30 a.m. During the nineteen years Elix and I had been together, this was the first time either one of us had lost a parent.

We arrived at Elix's mom's house around 6:30 in the morning. I was accompanied by emotions and feelings I never experienced before walking up the driveway. Elix's mom was very emotional when we walked into the house. Elix walked over to her and hugged her for several minutes while I just watched in tears. Once Elix let her go, I walked over to her and hugged her. I remember this hug was unlike any previous hug. I know Consuelo was very happy that we were there and would support her during this time.

One thing I didn't know was how different the services were in Puerto Rico compared to my experience of services in New England. The biggest difference was the wake. In Puerto Rico, it's not unusual for a wake to start around noon and end at ten, eleven, or twelve at night. Many of the funeral homes have dedicated rooms where there is coffee, tea, mini-sandwiches, and cookies for the immediate family and visitors. My experience with wakes was people coming in, paying respects to the family, sometimes sitting for a short period of time, and leaving. Also, the timeframe for a wake was usually no more than two or three hours. It was surprising to me that the family of the deceased would be at the funeral home for the wake for approximately ten hours.

I went with Elix to the funeral home to make the arrangements. The staff of the funeral home was empathetic and kind. Another thing that surprised me was when the funeral director told us Elix's dad would be embalmed within hours and suggested the wake be scheduled for the next day. I remember thinking, "Wow, that is fast," in my head when I heard the director state that. I knew Elix wanted this service to be a beautiful send-off to his dad and Elix did an incredible job making that happen.

There is a unique tree in Puerto Rico called **El Flamboyan,** Flamboyant Tree in English, also called a Royal Poinciana. The tree is often rated in the top five most beautiful flowering trees in the world. They usually bloom in or close to the month of June and the first time I saw one I was astounded by its beauty. The flowers come in a variety of colors such as red, orange, yellow, and the rarer blue. Elix knew his dad loved these trees and asked the funeral director if they could find blue flamboyant flowers for the casket. The director made no promises and said it wouldn't be easy because they are the rarest color. We finalized the plans and left the funeral home after about two hours. Around four hours later, Elix received a phone call from a staff member of the funeral home who told Elix they found the blue flamboyant flowers. We were both so happy.

The day of the wake was very long. We arrived at the funeral home at noon, and we left around 10 p.m. There were waves of people coming in to show their respects all day and people stayed at the funeral home for hours. Elix and I sneaked out of the funeral home around 6 p.m. and went to a sandwich shop to get something to eat. It was less about the food and more about needing some space away from the funeral home to breathe. Within forty-five minutes we were back and it did not appear that anyone knew we were gone.

A couple of times during the wake when I was sitting in the front row staring at the casket, I heard a voice that sounded like Servando's voice. My head would quickly look up at the casket and stare at Servo's body thinking how would I be able to hear his voice? Before we left the funeral home, the immediate family had a moment to go up to the casket and pay their last respects.

Elix and I got up together and I immediately started feeling waves of energy flowing through my body. I wasn't exactly sure what was going on, but I kept looking at Servo's body. I was staring at his face, and I thought I saw his head tilt a little and his eyes move a bit. I closed my eyes tightly for a second and opened them again. I stared at Servo's face again for at least one minute. His head did not move. I started questioning whether his head moved or if it was just my imagination. Part of me thought that would be impossible but the other part was certain that I saw his head and eyes move. I decided not to share this with Elix.

The following day we had to be at the funeral home at 9 a.m. for a brief service. Afterward, we would drive to the Veterans Cemetery in Bayamon, which was about one-and-a-half hours away from the funeral home. On the way to the cemetery, I was in the car with Elix when he started talking about his paternal grandfather whom I had never met. He told me his dad was a spitting image of his grandfather and he was happy that they were now together. We were traveling on the highway when I was looking out of the window, and something caught my eye. In the center of a tree that was facing the highway was a man's face. The tree was enormous with a trunk that was very large.

It happened quickly, but when I focused on the trunk of the tree, I saw a man's face with a hat on that looked like a fedora. Because the car was traveling so fast, I only had seconds to focus on the face on the tree. I looked at Elix and asked him, "Do you remember your grandfather ever wearing hats?" He responded saying his grandfather used to wear fedoras all the time and in the few pictures we have of him, he is wearing fedoras.

Did Elix's grandfather just show his face to me? Last night I thought I saw Elix's dad's head move, and now a face in the tree? What is going on with me? Am I going crazy? Little did I know, these experiences would make more sense in a couple of years.

INSIGHT

How can you tell if you are connecting with spirit or if it's the little voice in your head just chattering? This is the toughest question to answer because they are similar. Usually, a connection is something that comes out of nowhere. If you were having dinner with your girlfriend and as she was talking you saw cookies in your third eye or heard someone say cookies or just knew cookies were around, that random thought most likely is from spirit. If you pay attention, chances are your girlfriend at some point will bring up her grandmother, for instance, and talk about how she taught her how to make cookies. She also could just start talking about how much she loves and misses her grandmother, and I bet if you ask her did you guys bake cookies together, you will hear a loud yes!

CHAPTER 11

SPIRIT CONTINUES TO CONNECT

In September of 2012, three months after Elix's dad passed away, Elix and I traveled to Puerto Rico again. Everything was complete at the cemetery and Elix wanted to take his mom there to see the gravestone. It was early Monday morning and Elix and I went for a run before getting ready to head to the cemetery. When we got back to the house, Elix's mom was making us coffee, toast, and eggs. I was sitting at the living room table, listening to Elix and his mom talking in the kitchen, when I saw a turtle. Not a real turtle, but a snapshot or picture of a turtle in my mind. Was this my imagination? If it was, where did the turtle come from? I don't have any affiliation with turtles, nor had I seen any turtles in a long time.

Elix walked out of the kitchen with a cup of coffee for me and apparently, he could see the strange expression on my face. He put the cup down on the table and asked me what was going on. As crazy as I knew it would sound, I decided to tell Elix. I told him I saw a picture of a turtle in my mind, and he asked what I meant. I said it was hard to explain but it was like someone placed a picture of a turtle in front of my eyes, but it was in my imagination. Elix said it was weird, and I agreed.

We were meeting most of Elix's aunts at the cemetery at 1 p.m. When we arrived, it took us a bit to find the gravestone. We stopped at the office to pick up the description of the location of the grave. It had been three months since the last time we were at the cemetery and this cemetery is gigantic. After driving up and down many roads looking for the grave, we managed to find it. The three of us were standing in front of the grave when Elix's aunts pulled up. They all got out of their cars and met us with warm hugs. It was so nice seeing Servo's sisters at the cemetery and I knew it comforted Elix and his mom in this difficult situation.

Before we left the cemetery, everyone thought it would be a good idea to go to lunch. One of Elix's aunts selected a restaurant, and we decided to leave the cemetery and meet at this location. On the drive to the restaurant, one of Elix's aunts called Elix to tell him the restaurant we were planning to go to was closed on Mondays. Very quickly, Elix's aunt came up with another restaurant, so we changed the address in the GPS to the new location and started heading there.

Thirty minutes later we arrived at the restaurant. The parking lot was about half full and we found parking right away. The three of us got out of the car and started walking through the parking lot to the entrance of the restaurant. I looked up and I noticed something incredible. Adjacent to the front door of the restaurant was an enclosed koi pond, but it wasn't filled with koi, it was filled with turtles. The first thought that popped into my head was, **Turtles again?** For the next few minutes, I tried to make sense of the turtle vision from this morning and the turtles in the pond. Was this just a coincidence? Later I would learn from spirit that there is no such thing as a coincidence.

Did Elix's dad show me a turtle because he knew we would end up at this restaurant with the pond of turtles? No, that is crazy. How would a dead person show me a picture of a turtle that was connected to a restaurant we would go to? How would he know we would end up at this restaurant? We weren't even supposed to go to this restaurant. During lunch, I brought up the turtles at the restaurant and my vision of a turtle this morning, and asked Elix if he thought they were related. Elix said he thought there was a good chance they were related, and it would be nice to think that his dad was responsible for it and still around.

Elix and I had decided to stay at the Ponce Hilton, which was only about five minutes from his mom's house. In case there were any family members that wanted to stay over at Consuelo's house while we were visiting, it would be easier to have us stay close by.

I ALWAYS LOVED THE IDEA THAT I MIGHT HAVE A GUARDIAN ANGEL. Prior to going to Puerto Rico, I was searching for a book to read on spirit. I didn't know much about the spirit world and thought some insight may help me. One chapter of the book I was reading was called "Meeting Your Spirit Guides." It was so cool to think that all of us have spirit guides who help us navigate this journey, and if we could personally meet them (well, not in person), I'm all in for that.

One morning during our trip to Puerto Rico, Elix and I went outside to exercise. Our routine was to run on the path that followed the perimeter of the hotel. Elix would add in other cardio elements, so I was usually done exercising first and would head to the room to take a shower. That morning, I finished first and headed for the room. The night before I had been reading my book and there was an exercise in the chapter on how to meet your spirit guide or angel. The exercise instructed you to take some deep breaths, meditate for a period of time, and ask your spirit guides to appear. Ask them for his or her name, or names if there is more than one. The book was very clear that this may take a long time before something may happen and if it doesn't, still know that your guides are still present.

Up until this point, I had been doing the same meditation every day. It was about eighteen minutes long and I thought it was good. It was a guided meditation so I would use my headphones while meditating and always took several deep breaths before I started. It was especially beautiful meditating here because we were on the top floor of the hotel in a room with a balcony. Going on the balcony and sitting in one of the chairs with an ocean view was breathtaking. Beautiful palm trees swaying back and forth, the smell of the ocean, and nothing but the sounds of the waves crashing into the shoreline. I loved it when we stayed there.

I finished my meditation and before I opened my eyes, I asked my spirit guide to appear to me. I honestly had no expectations, and I wasn't really sure if anything would happen, but I thought I'll do this anyway. I opened my eyes slowly and my focus was drawn to the sky immediately. I couldn't believe my eyes. In front of me, in the sky, was a cloud that looked exactly like Jesus, with his arms stretched out, flying through the sky. Is Jesus my guardian angel? It was one of the most beautiful things I had ever seen.

I thought, *I need to take a picture of this, but where is my phone?* I ran into the hotel room, grabbed my cell phone from the bed, and ran back outside on the balcony hoping the cloud formation didn't change. If anything, when I focused the camera on my phone to the cloud, it looked even better. I took about ten pictures of the cloud, trying to get every angle. As the cloud eventually changed shape, I stood on the balcony, staring into the ocean thinking I had just met my guardian angel and he was real. As soon as Elix returned to the room, I explained to him the exercise I followed and the picture. He was amazed when he looked at the photo and could not believe how much it looked like Jesus with this welcoming pose.

My Guardian Angel in the Sky

SPIRIT CONTINUES TO CONNECT

That evening when we returned to the hotel for the night, we were lying in bed watching TV and I thought it would be a good time to tell Elix about my vision right before his dad passed away. I told him I saw a man, grabbing his neck and collapsing to the floor. I also showed him the email I sent myself back in June stating what I had just told him. I remember Elix looking at me and saying that was the description of exactly what happened to my dad right before he passed away. Elix continued and said, "You saw what was going to happen to my dad a day before it happened." I think for both of us, this conversation brought us to a better level of understanding of the spirit world, but also made us realize that there is so much more that we didn't know.

I WISH I HAD ANOTHER MEDIUM TO TALK TO. In February 2013, Elix and I stopped in Shaw's supermarket to get a couple of things. As we were walking in the market, I looked up and saw a friend of Elix's, John Harvey. Elix had been friends with him for many years but hadn't seen him in a long time. I met John once back in 1995 when Elix and I had bought our first home. Elix told me a friend of his, who is a Medium, was going to stop over to see the new house. I was very intrigued but didn't know anything about Mediums at that point. He arrived at the house and Elix opened the front door to let him in. He had a beautiful presence and was so kind and friendly. He loved the house and told us what he was picking up as a psychic Medium. He told us he saw a dog in the house, who will have lots of shedding and is blond or light tan.

He also mentioned that there were water issues in the house and that the couple that owned the house previously had one child. As soon as he talked about the dog, Elix and I looked at each other with a surprised look. When we came to see the house when it was still furnished and the previous owners were still living there, we saw a picture of their dog who was a large blond dog. In discussions with the couple, they also told us they had one daughter. We didn't validate the water issue because we had the house inspected and water issues did not come up in the inspector's report. I was taken aback by how accurate John was and thought to myself, **Boy, I wish I could do that.**

About two months into living in the new house, there was a day that it was raining from morning until night. The house was a ranch with a finished basement. I went downstairs for something and as I was heading back upstairs, right before I got to the staircase, I realized my foot felt wet. I looked down and then squatted to feel the floor and yelled to Elix, "Come down here quickly." Water was entering the basement floor and the rug was damp. Over the next year, whenever it rained steadily water would seep into the basement floor. We are not sure how the inspector didn't catch that, but the person who validated it was John Harvey the Medium. Eventually, we installed a retaining wall which resolved the water issue, but John was three for three in his validations.

John wasn't looking in our direction in the supermarket, but I told Elix, "Isn't that your friend John?" Elix yelled out "John!" and with a big smile on his face, he came running up to Elix and me and gave us both a big hug. At that point, we had been in our new house for about eight years and John told us he was living in the same town. After the initial catching up, John looked at me and said, "There is a big white light behind you with all your loved ones in spirit standing there. They are so proud of you... and who is Stanley?" I told him he is my uncle who passed away and John told me he is always around me and guiding me. He also told Elix that he had a lot of loved ones around him, and they protected him. I briefly told John about what was going on with me and the Mediumship, and he was excited. We exchanged emails and selected a Friday night in the following weeks for John to come to our house for dinner.

Before we left John, he said to me, "Steven I can't wait to hear what is going on with you and your spirit journey and I'm excited to help you in any way I can." I was so excited about this dinner! About one week later, we confirmed our dinner date with John, and he responded how excited he was to see our new house and that we lived so close to each other.

On the Monday before the dinner date on Friday, I emailed John to make sure he had our address, and that dinner was happening. I realized on Wednesday I never received a response from John, so I told Elix and Elix emailed him that Wednesday. The rest of the day went by, and by Thursday, still no response. Friday morning Elix sent another email and called John but no response. Friday came and went, and we never heard from John. The following Monday morning, I was driving to court for a hearing and a truck entered the highway and managed to ride parallel to me. I looked at the truck and, on the side, printed was the name "Harvey." That was John's last name and the second I saw the name, an uneasy feeling rushed through my entire body. I called Elix on my cell phone and told him what just happened and that something was not right. Unfortunately, without John responding to the emails, we couldn't validate anything.

A couple of hours later, Elix called me. I could tell right away that he had some unpleasant news. Elix told me he found the email address of a friend of John's and sent him a message asking him if he was still in touch with John. John's friend responded that John passed away from a sudden heart attack last Tuesday. My heart sank to my feet when I heard the news.

Elix and I went to John's funeral the following day. When we were driving home, I asked Elix if he remembered John saying in the supermarket that his lack of confidence always prevented him from doing more with his gift. It was hard to reconcile that statement because John's gift was tremendous. Right at that moment, I could feel John letting me know he would be my guide and what he wanted to accomplish in his lifetime, he would accomplish working with me as my partner. John was taken too soon from us, but I have included him in my daily meditation since he passed away.

OUR DOGS ARE OUR CHILDREN. In May 2013, I was bringing up the patio furniture from the basement to the deck. We had three dogs at that time: Rico, Little Ricky, and Memphis, a.k.a. Monkey. Rico was in the house eating a cookie and the other two were on the deck with me. I realized I left my phone in the kitchen, so I stepped into the kitchen from the deck and grabbed it from the island. I turned around and headed back outside on the deck and when I was just about to step onto the deck, I heard, "Look up now." I looked up immediately and there was a hawk right above me, no more than ten feet above my head. I screamed, I waved my arms, my phone went flying out of my hand, and the hawk started flapping his wings faster to fly away from the deck. It was like it was happening in slow motion and I could hear the sound of the hawk's wings flapping as it flew back into the sky. I knew the hawk was coming down for one of the boys and when I screamed, Monkey ran into the house.

The patio furniture was in several pieces that you had to connect, and the separate pieces were spread across the deck. Little Ricky is ten pounds, so it was easy for him to hide behind one of the pieces of patio furniture. Ultimately, I found him behind a chair, grabbed him, and went inside. I counted all three dogs inside and then broke down and started crying. I knew how close I came to having a hawk either carry Little Ricky away or hurt him or even kill him. Then I remembered the voice that said look up now. I asked spirit who yelled that out and I kept hearing a "B" name like Barbara or Beatrice. Neither one of those names connected with me. When Elix got home, I asked him if either of those B names meant anything to him and he said of course, that's his aunt in spirit that was like a second mother to him. I looked at him and said but her name was Taity. Elix responded that that was her nickname, but her first name was Beatrice. I had never heard him refer to his aunt by that name. I thanked her for saving little Ricky. She was the closest person to Elix and she is also his number one fan and guardian.

INSIGHT

I have learned from spirit that there are no such things as coincidences or mistakes. Everything happens the way it is supposed to happen, and spirit plays a big part in this. Whether it's good or bad, once you believe that everything does happen for a reason, your connection to spirit gets much stronger.

CHAPTER 12

MY FIRST READING

It was February 2013, and I was in the house waiting for a guy to come fix the garage door. Three days before I had backed out of the garage before the door was completely open, collided with it, and dented the door. It would only close if you gave it assistance and really pushed it down. The guy showed up and looks like he is six feet four, has a full beard, and his arms are the size of my head. He introduced himself as Shawn and started working on the garage door. I went upstairs and told him to call me when he was finished. About forty-five minutes later, I heard him shouting up to me to say he was done. I came back down, and he explained to me what he did to fix the door. As he is talking to me, the above mechanism that opens and closes the garage door made the loudest noise I had ever heard. The steel wire in the mechanism was shaking but the garage door never moved. Both of us jumped at the noise and I yelled, "What was that!" He said in twenty-plus years of doing this work, he had never seen or heard anything like what just happened. Shawn checked everything and made the door go up and down several times, but there appeared to be no issues.

After spending some more time looking things over, he told me everything was working great and told me how much the fee would be. I ran upstairs to my office to write out a check. After I wrote the check and was heading back down to the garage, I heard a woman's voice saying, "Just say the "A" name." I knew it was spirit for Shawn but didn't have any idea what to do with the A name. Shawn was very intimidating solely by his size even though he was a really nice guy. I handed Shawn the check as he was writing out the paid invoice for me. I got up the nerve and asked Shawn if there was someone connected to him that had a name that started with an "A." He stared at me, never asked me why I was asking him that, and then responded, "I don't think so." I said that's okay, sometimes I get feelings and hear things, and it felt like it was someone that is dead but was very close to you. He handed me the invoice and walked out of the garage and got into his truck.

I was about to go upstairs but spirit was very persistent. Something made me walk up to his truck as he was sitting in the driveway and said to him, "Shawn, are you sure you don't have someone dead with the "A" name?" He responded with well yes, but she died a long time ago. I told him the timeframe didn't matter and asked who was the "A." He looked at me and said eighteen years ago he lost his mom whom he was very close to, and her name was Anita. I told him she just wanted to let you know she is still with you and proud of you. He stared back at me for a couple of seconds with his eyes getting glossy and said, "That was cool." He pulled out of the driveway, and I closed the garage door and went upstairs. I realized that was the first time I had ever read someone, and it felt amazing. I asked spirit that night why my first read was a guy that could crush me in about one minute and then laughed. Little did I know how significant this first reading with just one letter would be.

Starting in 2013, I registered for various classes to be able to learn everything I could about the spirit world. After my Medium certification class, I also completed a Clairvoyance Class, Psychic Class, Past-Lives Class, Spirit Attachments Class and completed the three levels of Reiki study to become a Reiki Master. Clairvoyance is the ability to connect with spirit through seeing or visions. All the ways a Medium or psychic connects with spirit are classified by the *clairs.* Clairaudience is the ability to connect with spirit by hearing information. Clairsentience is the ability to connect with spirit by a strong feeling or strong sensing. There are many more *clairs*, but this gives you an idea that each person is different in how they receive information from spirit.

After I conquered my fear of approaching people with the reading of Shawn, in the following months I would randomly read people. Sometimes it would be in court, in the supermarket, in the mall, or whenever I felt that spirit had something to say to the person who was near me. It was a great way to practice, and the love I had for it was a motivator to keep on doing informal readings. However, there were many times that I would start doing a reading, and most of the things I said were not validated by the person I was reading. When those experiences occurred, I would be very hard on myself and become very withdrawn. I would start questioning myself on the degree of what I thought was my gift and sometimes wonder if it went away. The interesting part of this process was it never stopped me from doing my next reading.

This industry or profession is very similar to an acting environment. I believe you must have thick skin, be confident, and always trust yourself. It was a roller coaster ride for me, and I quickly realized I was only as good as my last reading. Thankfully, most of the people I read were very receptive to the process, regardless of whether they validated information on the spot or not. There were a couple of times the person I approached would say they were not interested in a reading, but when you walk up to someone you don't know, it's hard to know how they will react. In hindsight, I believe spirit guided me to people who were open and really needed to hear from their loved ones. Currently, I can usually sense whether a person will be receptive or not.

Just like how individuals are different in how they get their information from spirit, individuals are also different in how they do readings. There are some Mediums that believe walking up to a stranger and reading them is intrusive and they won't do that. I trust spirit and know if I am being nudged to do an impromptu reading, the person really needs to get the message. Just like any profession, not all people are going to agree on how the process should work. This is not an easy industry to work in and it's great when you feel support from others, regardless of how different the process may be for them.

One thing that surprised me was the number of letters, emails, and cards I received from people whom I read. I have saved every one of them. There have been a lot of tears and hugs from people that I read, but I have never experienced the overwhelming satisfaction I feel after seeing the transformation of the person I just read. I can feel the person's energy is so much lighter and more at peace.

It was also a very interesting time for me because my law practice was at its peak so I was busy traveling to several courts per week, but now I also had spirit to contend with. Working as both an attorney and a Medium didn't really flow too well. I spent much of my day in court, either Probate or Juvenile, and that atmosphere is a very controlled, conservative place. Sitting next to attorneys waiting for my case to be called and hearing a voice saying, "The woman sitting next to you is my daughter, please let her know I am here," isn't what most attorneys are dealing with.

SPIRIT DID NOT PREPARE me for this day. I had to be in Probate Court at 9 a.m. for a hearing. When the hearing was over, I went to the scheduling department before I left to schedule another hearing. The receptionist was on the phone when I entered the room and there were two court employees at their desks talking to each other. As I was waiting, I heard a baby laughing. I could tell there was a baby girl in spirit that was with me, and she was connected to one of the two women sitting at their desks. I walked over to the other side of the room and introduced myself as Attorney Macek.

I then asked them how either of them was connected to a little girl who had crossed over and there is an "S" name connected. Both expressions on their faces dramatically changed and one of them started crying. The woman who was not crying looked at me and said, "She just lost her granddaughter who was two years old, why would you bring that up?" At this point, the woman who lost her granddaughter was crying a lot and a court officer entered the room to see what was going on. I was so taken aback and told the ladies that I was sorry, I connect to spirit sometimes and I could hear a young girl laughing in spirit and she wanted to tell you she is okay.

The court officer started walking over to me and said it's time you left. The woman who was crying said no, I want to talk to him. She introduced herself to me and said her granddaughter passed away three months ago and her name was Shannon. She also asked me, "Did you say she is okay?" I told her yes and she kisses her brother every night before he goes to bed. I then apologized again for my approach, and she motioned for me to go out of the door I came in, and told me to go to the other door to this room. I did, and she was at the entrance to the door to meet me. She hugged me and said she needed so badly to know her granddaughter was not alone and was okay.

The court officer was still suspiciously looking at me when I left, and I never scheduled the hearing I originally went in there for. I left the courthouse and when I got to my car, I just sat there, and tears started rolling down my face. I was angry and started yelling at spirit. Why would you not tell me this little girl passed away so recently? Why didn't you give me a heads up? How could you just have me start talking about this little girl without a better introduction to who I was? At that point, I realized I had so much to learn about the spirit world.

I didn't have a website in 2013 so I started advertising readings on my Facebook page. In September 2013, a woman sent me a message via Facebook asking to set up a reading. I responded and we set the date for October 9, 2013. This was going to be my first formal reading. At that point, I did not have an office because my legal work didn't require one. For Juvenile Court I visited my clients at their homes and for Probate Court, hospitals, and nursing homes would fax me the required documents I needed so I never had a need to rent an office. We made plans for me to go to my client's home, which was in Rhode Island.

We were living in Norton, Massachusetts, so the Rhode Island border was about fifteen minutes away. I don't think I slept much of the evening on October 8 because I knew this person was paying me so the standard was much higher, and I also wanted to do a great job so she would recommend me. What would happen if no spirits came through when I started the reading? I arrived at her home and the reading was for one hour. I brought a notebook and a pen just in case I needed to jot something down. At the end of the reading, she was very happy and told me she really enjoyed the reading. I left there so relieved but also so proud that I just did a reading for one hour.

Over the following year, I did a lot of traveling. A few months after my first formal reading, a woman booked a reading for three people. I remember talking to Elix about how I was going to read three people. Three people are too many for me to read. I came very close to canceling the appointment, but I ultimately decided to do my best and keep it. It was a married couple and the mother of the wife, and we sat at their dining room table. There were some big validations throughout the reading, but I also went over the hour it was scheduled for; I believe the entire reading lasted for one and a half hours. I had the need to make sure there were enough validations for all three before I could stop. This was primarily due to my lack of confidence and trust in myself, which made me focus more on whether someone liked the reading or not. All three of them were very satisfied after the reading was completed.

As time moved on, I was getting busier with appointments. I would take any appointments, regardless of where the person was located. If I didn't want to travel, the only other way to do a reading was to have the person or people come to my house. This wasn't a perfect plan, but it saved me from continuously traveling around and I was traveling a lot.

One of the problems with having people come to our house was if Elix was home, he would have to go upstairs and bring our dogs with him. If I had an appointment at 5 p.m then Elix would have to eat early or after 6 p.m. Sometimes I would have two people coming together with back-to-back one-hour readings which would force Elix to be upstairs for at least two hours. In addition, there was a risk of having strangers over at our house and having our address known to many people.

One evening, two women came to the house for a one-hour reading. When that occurred, I did my best to give thirty minutes to one person and the other thirty minutes to the other person. I started with the first woman and about ten minutes into the reading, a grandmother in spirit started coming through. I remember telling her there is a grandmother here and she smiled. I then asked her who had the "M" name like Mary or Marilyn and the smile instantly went away. She said her paternal grandmother's name was Madeline and she wanted her to go away and not return. She told me she has nothing to say to her. That had never happened to me up until that point, and I got somewhat flustered. I then asked that grandmother to honor her granddaughter's wishes, but she wouldn't budge. I could tell she was not leaving until she said her piece. I also realized that unless she agreed to step aside, no one else in spirit was going to come through.

I tried my best to explain what was happening and my client agreed to hear what her grandmother wanted to say. The grandmother started apologizing and taking responsibility for her actions while here on earth. My client sat and listened, and a couple of times her eyes filled up with tears. She told me at the end of the reading that her paternal grandmother had disowned her mom's side of the family and caused a lot of hurt for her and her mom. A couple of weeks later, my client emailed me to tell me she told her mom what occurred in the reading, and after processing it, they both felt like they were in a better place. I was so happy and relieved when I read her message.

INSIGHT

Practice, practice, practice. Just like any gift or talent, the only way to hone in on the Mediumship skill is to practice. Your friends and family are the best people to practice with whether using tarot cards or straight Mediumship. Social media is another helpful tool for practicing. There are so many Medium/psychic Facebook pages to join, which allow you to offer readings to participants on that page. The feedback is instrumental to the growth of your gift. Always remember, there will be mistakes with the people you read. Many times, that is not due to your reading, it's due to the recipient innocently not connecting the information or remembering a particular experience. Practicing increased my connection to spirit immensely.

CHAPTER 13

BRANCHING OUT

After doing months of readings in my home, I decided it was time to start looking for an office of my own. I did research online to see what was available, knowing I needed a small office that I could afford. I found an office in Mansfield that was in the basement of this three-story office building. The amazing thing about this office was it was five minutes from my home. I met a representative of the property management team, and he showed me the office. There was a main lobby with four other single offices off this lobby. I wasn't thrilled with a basement office, but it did have a window which, in my eyes, was necessary to consider taking the office.

It was tiny, but a great first office. I took pictures of the office and lobby and asked the representative about the other tenants. The other tenants traveled for their business, so they weren't in their office full time. I told my husband about it that night and decided to rent the office! I was very happy (and stressed) about the new monthly expense, but I was determined to do more readings to cover the extra costs.

Moving into the office was easy because it was so small. I bought a small, white progressive desk with no drawers, several chairs I could stack, and some decorative paintings and floor items to make the office look comfortable. I was so excited when I booked my first reading and I could give the person my office address. Elix was also very pleased that his day wasn't interrupted at home anymore.

After being in that office for one year, I was looking to upgrade and get out of the basement office. Next to the building where my office was located, there was a two-story building that was owned by the same management company. I noticed that there was a first-floor office that would be available soon, so I asked to see it. The rent was higher but unlike my one- room office, this one had two rooms. The big part of the office was an open space, then there was a door that led into a smaller office that had a window. I could have larger groups in the big room, which was great, but I did not like that the bigger room did not have any windows. However, it got me out of the basement so I moved in.

One year after moving in, I was notified that the buildings were sold and there would be new landlords. I met with one of the new representatives, and my rent was increased way too much from what it was worth for the square footage of that office. I decided not to sign a new lease and started looking for a new office. Prior to looking for available offices, I meditated and asked my paternal grandmother, Rose, to help me find an office that worked for me. I also asked all my business office guides for help in spirit. We have our loved ones in spirit that are close to us all the time, however we also have guides and angels with us. What most people don't realize is there is always a specific, very focused spirit at our disposal.

As a lawyer, when I had a tough hearing, right before the hearing I would ask for my attorney spirits to be with me, guide me, and help me. I would only tune in to the individuals that previously walked this earth, were attorneys, and were experts at what they did. When you ask, they listen and do whatever they can to help you. That works across the board whether you are a dentist, cosmetologist, race car driver, etc.

The first office I found online sounded great. It was in Stoughton, which was about twenty-five minutes from my home. Certainly not as convenient as the Mansfield office, but I made an appointment to see it. As I was almost there, I noticed the street over from the street the office was on was called Rose Glen. I knew that was my grandmother Rose answering my plea for assistance. I met the owner of the building who showed me the office.

The office was on the second floor (this was a two-story building) and it was a corner office. The office had two rooms, a smaller one with one window and a bigger room with several windows. Because it was a corner office, it had its own private entrance. I loved it instantly. I told the owner I wanted to bring my husband back to look at it, which we did the same week. I then called the owner to let him know I would be taking it and I signed the lease. In March 2018, I moved into the office in Stoughton.

MY GOAL WAS TO DO A LARGE GROUP EVENT. As the months went by, I continued to do private readings in my office as well as group readings in people's homes. Lisa, a server at this restaurant in Rhode Island we frequented, booked an appointment for a reading with her sister. Both of them loved their readings. Several weeks later, we went to this restaurant and Lisa asked me a question. She told me about a restaurant about five minutes away that had a function room where people held events. She wanted to know if I would be interested in doing a Medium event in this function room. I was very excited and said yes, I would be very interested. She texted me the owner's name of the restaurant and the following day I reached out to her. Immediately after I told Lisa yes, I started second- guessing myself and thinking about what I had gotten myself into.

The restaurant was Uncle Ronnie's Tavern and the owner, Paula, was very nice. We selected the date for the event of November 30, 2015. Paula only wanted to accept cash to purchase tickets, which made getting tickets harder because people would have to go to the restaurant to pick them up. It was my first event, so I was agreeable with anything she wanted to ensure the event happened. Paula wasn't well-versed in marketing events, so I did my best on social media to advertise and have people share my posts. The goal was to get as many attendees as I could, but I did not have a particular number of attendees in mind.

On the morning of November 30, the number of attendees was fifty. This was overwhelming for me and the night before I barely slept. The room for events was downstairs and it had a separate entrance from the restaurant upstairs. Elix and I got there about one hour before the event started; there was a very small private room that I could go into until Elix announced that the event was starting. I was sitting in this small room with headphones on listening to music. Music has always been my muse and not only makes me feel wonderful, but also lifts my energy closer to the frequency of spirit.

Elix popped his head into the small room and told me I had about ten minutes left. After he left, I tuned into spirit and asked my two grandmothers, Rose and Anna, for help and I asked them to please be with me for support.

Ten minutes later, Elix opened the door to the small room and said, "It's showtime." I took a deep breath and said, "C'mon grandmas, it's time." I was very nervous and just wanted to be able to connect people with their loved ones in spirit. I did my introduction and was ready to start my first reading.

I remember a young man in spirit standing next to me who said, "My mom is here, just bring up the bridge." I told the audience about the young man, and a woman held her hand up. I walked up to her and asked her if she lost a young man and she said yes, her son jumped off a bridge to end his life.

I then got even closer to her and asked her what her name was. She answered Rose. Immediately I knew it was my grandmother Rose, letting me know she was with me. That moment made me feel so good and I let go of a lot of my nerves. The reading with Rose was incredible and her son did such a great job letting her know he was okay, how much he loved her, and how he was always with her. Rose cried a lot, but they were happy tears and she was able to let go of a lot of guilty feelings she had held on to for many years.

The next reading was with a dad in spirit who repeatedly told me he died quickly and there were questions surrounding his death. When I announced that, a woman raised her hand and told me that her dad went into the hospital for a routine procedure and died during it. She also said there are so many unanswered questions that she thinks about every day. I walked over to her and asked her what her name was. She responded with Anna. I was in shock, my other grandmother.

At that point, I was so excited that I stopped the reading and told the audience that I asked my two grandmothers, Rose, and Anna, to be with me tonight and the first two readings were for Rose and Anna. I could hear gasps through the room with one woman near me saying, "I have goosebumps." The rest of Anna's reading was spectacular, and so many of her loved ones came through in such a quick period.

The event lasted two hours and seeing close friends of mine sprinkled throughout the audience was so calming. When the event was over, I was bombarded with people coming up to me and asking me questions. Of course there were many questions from the people that I didn't get to read, like does my father, mother, etc. have any messages for me. After about ten minutes, Elix came swooping in and told the people talking to me and waiting to talk to me that I had to go, then thanked everyone again for coming to the event. Elix is one of a kind and is always taking care of me and protecting me. I didn't think about who would introduce me at the beginning of the event, and he just took that on himself. He also included information about me and made me sound wonderful. He is the most supportive person in the world and will do anything for me.

INSIGHT

*What is important? Over the years of doing readings, there have been a handful of spirits that have told me of regrets they have. When we cross over, we get to see what I call the **blueprint of life**. This starts from when we are born and continues until we cross over. We see how we lived our lives, our choices and decisions, how we treated people, how we treated ourselves, and the effect we had on other people. Two common themes I have heard from spirit are: I didn't spend enough time with the people I love, and I didn't do what I wanted to do in life. Spirit reminds me all the time how fast this experience on earth goes by and to do what makes you happy. The only way to truly be happy and get what you want is by taking risks and believing in yourself. This is what I believe to be most important in this life.*

CHAPTER 14

IT'S ALL IN THE "GENES"

Somebody once said to me, "A Medium is always a psychic, but a psychic is not always a Medium." A Medium connects with the energy of the loved ones in spirit that are connected to the person they are reading. When I do a reading, the person's mother, father, grandparent, brother, etc. will come through to connect with the person. I also connect with the energy of the person in front of me.

A psychic connects with the energy of the person they are reading. Most of a psychic's information comes from the person in front of them. If a psychic validates something about the person's grandmother in spirit, chances are the person they are reading is thinking about their grandmother and that is where the psychic is extracting the information.

Once I realized I was a Medium, in addition to taking courses I also read several books written by other Mediums. One common trait I read in most of the books was that Mediums would talk about how their mother, grandmother, or grandfather were also Mediums or psychics. It was very interesting to me, and I wondered if every Medium or psychic has someone in their family tree who is also gifted. Is that where it comes from? Does it skip generations? Can one sibling have it and the other not? I had so many questions because it was so incredibly interesting to me. It also gave me the idea to ask my family about our family tree.

I talked to Elix one night and told him I was going to ask my mom and aunt if they were aware of any family members that were connected to spirit. He thought it was a great idea. One night, the four of us went out to dinner, and I asked them both what they knew of the spirit world. My mother and aunt looked at me for a second, with expressions on their faces like I was crazy, and then it was like the floodgates opened. Very nonchalantly, my aunt said, "Oh, Mama was an amazing psychic. People would come from other towns to see her and get a reading." My mom said that my maternal grandmother, Anna, would use a deck of playing cards to read people. They weren't tarot cards, just a regular set of playing cards. Somehow my grandmother labeled all fifty-two cards with messages and could read someone and their future with that deck. I think my mouth stayed open for about five minutes listening to the two of them chatter about my grandmother. My aunt Dolores was the youngest of the four daughters, and periodically I would hear her mention that she liked witches and magic. She once told me that she tried to do some spells using parchment paper and recited some words and said she was successful, and the spells worked.

Once the two of them paused about this subject, I asked them both why neither one of them ever talked about my grandmother being a psychic. They both responded that there was no specific reason why they never mentioned it, only that the subject never came up. This information made me feel even more connected to spirit, but also created so many more questions. My mom and aunt also mentioned that my grandfather, Fredrick (my middle name), yelled at my grandmother when she read people. He would say that people were going to think she was a witch if she continued doing that "magic stuff."

My grandmother would tell him she would stop, but when he went to work during the day, she would have people come over so she could read them. My mom or my other two aunts, Alma and Rita, never mentioned anything to me about spirit. My mom was always a believer in spirit but never talked about any experiences, except saying she would feel my dad in the house.

It was always strange to me that my paternal grandmother, Rose, was the grandmother always with me in spirit and not the psychic grandmother, Anna. My mother was always very vocal about how close she was to her father, Fred. She told me many times over the years that his nickname for her was "Partner." As teenagers, my other three aunts started smoking but my mom never smoked. She would tell me her dad would say to her "Partner, if I ever see you smoke, that will be it."

My mother loved both her parents very much. As I've mentioned, she also loved her three sisters, and they were close all their lives. My mom once told me a story that when she was younger, she got her mother, Anna, upset about something and Anna took off her shoe and threw it at my mom. I never liked that story, and it made me more of a fan of Fred and not Anna. Up until six months ago, I started wondering if that was partly the reason why I have always been so close to my paternal grandmother Rose and not Anna. I decided to meditate one day and had a conversation with my grandmother, Anna. I told her how much I love her, and I am sorry if that shoe-throwing story altered my feelings for her over the years. I got chills through my body after stating that to her and I knew it was her soul hugging me.

INSIGHT

I am not totally sure how much genetics play a role in a person being a Medium or psychic or highly sensitive to the spirit world. I do believe it's necessary to acknowledge your family tree whether you know some of them or not. There is always a percentage of genes that we get from our grandparents, great-grandparents, great-great grandparents, etc., and thanking them and validating that they are still around you is one of the best things someone can do to be more connected.

CHAPTER 15

EXPOSURE

At some point, I started to think about exposure and what I could do to be visible to more people and get the opportunity to do more readings. One Sunday morning, in April 2017, I was sitting in my living room with the dogs and reading *The Boston Globe*. Elix was still sleeping. In the Style Section of the newspaper, there was an interesting article about a woman who changed careers after many years to do what she loved, and her new business was flourishing.

I read the article and at the end, the writer's name was listed. His first name was Paul and his email was listed also. I thought, **What if I email him, explain my story about the Mediumship, and see if he's interested in doing an article on me?** To sweeten the pot, I also included that I would be happy to give him a reading in exchange for having an article written about me. That morning I emailed Paul, jotting down a snapshot of my life, and crossed my fingers as I hit the send button.

A couple of days later, I received an email from Paul. He was very interested in my story and asked me about getting a reading. I suggested that we meet in my office; I would give him a reading and then he could interview me for the article for the **Boston Globe**. I proposed going first because I knew I would be nervous reading the guy that would write an article about me, and I wanted to get it over with so I could concentrate on the interview.

It was a Saturday, late morning, and Paul arrived at my office. He was very nice and appeared to be a laid-back kind of guy. I told him I would read him first and then we could do the interview portion. I had gotten into the habit of using my iPhone to do an audio recording of the reading. People loved it because after the reading, I would email the recording to them, and they could listen to it and keep it forever.

Paul's loved ones did a fabulous job at coming through and giving Paul incredible validation. He responded to my email stating he loved the reading and couldn't wait for his family to listen to it.

During the next five months, Paul and I would exchange emails about his interview with me. I had to provide him with a variety of pictures, and one or more would be included in *The Boston Globe* article. I was so anxious about the article appearing in the paper and I was getting very impatient as the months went by.

At the beginning of August 2017, Paul told me that my article would be in the Sunday edition and could be in the paper as soon as that week. Paul was a freelance writer so he never had definite information about when something would appear in the paper until the last minute. Every Sunday I would race to the nearest store to purchase *The Boston Globe*. Week after week, no article.

On September 16, 2017, Elix and I invited our very good friends, Pam and Bill, to come over for dinner. Pam owned a cabin in Sedgwick, Maine, which was breathtaking. We drove up to the cabin the year before and stayed there for four days. There is nothing but woods, nature, and beauty in every direction you turn when you are there. In the several years we went up there, we saw bears, deer, and so much other wonderful wildlife.

As we were finishing dinner in the dining room, Elix was talking about the article in *The Boston Globe* that will be coming out one of these upcoming Sundays. Bill mentioned that you can access some of what's in the Sunday newspaper on Saturday night online. I had never heard that, so I grabbed my phone and immediately went to *TheBoston Globe's* website. I put in "Steven the Medium" in the search vehicle and my article popped up! It was there, in the newspaper! I pushed the seat back that I was sitting on in the dining room and jumped up and down with excitement. "It's finally here, it's finally here," I belted out. I was acting like a five-year-old boy who just got a Christmas present. I couldn't help it, it was a long time waiting.

Within one minute, all four of us were on our phones, pulling up the article and reading it. I had no idea which picture they would use, and they used one of me sitting at a table, from that past Easter. I was dressed up in a jacket and I really liked the picture.

On September 17, 2017, the next day, I did not go to the store early in the morning. As much as I was so excited to hold the actual paper, I wanted to go to the store with

Elix. Elix drove into the store parking lot, and I ran into the store. I grabbed six papers and ran to the cashier to pay for them. I didn't start digging through the paper to see the article because I wanted to be sitting next to Elix so we could both see it together.

When I got back into the car, Elix was just waiting for me. I started shuffling through the paper because I was looking for the particular section that I knew my article would be in. I found the section and started turning each page looking for my article as Elix watched me. I turned to the next page and there it was. I looked at the article and screamed out, "It's a different picture and it's the one with Jango!" I never thought the picture online would be different from the one in hard print.

We had three dogs at that time, all Japanese Chins: Little Ricky, Memphis (a.k.a. Monkey) and Jango. One of the pictures I submitted to Paul was one of me holding Jango at the veterinarian's office. It was perfect on so many levels. Being an animal advocate and having rescued all three of these dogs and treating them as family, made this the perfect choice.

I couldn't wait to show everyone I knew, to email everyone I knew, and to post it on social media. It was the first time I was in print in reference to being a Medium, and it made me feel that everything was moving forward with the spirit world.

In November 2017, I received a phone call from a representative from *Massachusetts Lawyers Weekly* periodical. *Massachusetts Lawyers Weekly* is a prominent newspaper for the legal community, locally and nationally. The representative asked me if I would be interested in being profiled in the paper. He said I would be the first attorney/Medium ever appearing in the periodical. I was shocked, surprised, and very emotional when I realized what he was asking me.

Massachusetts Lawyers Weekly is the newspaper that every law student learns about and utilizes throughout school and beyond. It has an outstanding reputation in the legal community. I had a subscription, like a lot of students, during law school and maintained that subscription for many years in the legal workforce. The representative asked me to send him a biography and any information I thought would be pertinent to be profiled as an attorney/Medium. I started that assignment immediately and had Elix review the document before I sent it to the representative.

January 11, 2018, *Massachusetts Lawyers Weekly* was out and distributed and I was profiled in the paper. It was a great article. I was working in both Probate and Juvenile Court at the time and in both venues, the number of attorneys coming up to me and congratulating me felt endless. It was officially known that I was not just an attorney, but a Medium also.

It was so interesting how some attorneys had so many questions about me being a Medium: how did I find out, how long had I known, and the big question, "Does spirit tell you if your clients or the defense are lying?" Some attorneys congratulated me and then got away from me quickly. It's sometimes common for people to be nervous around Mediums because they think their loved ones in spirit will give them bad information or are upset with them or some people are skeptics.

I HAD WANTED TO DO A FUNDRAISER FOR DOGS. It was March 2018, and I was talking to my cousin/sister Holly, who lives in Florida. Our family has always been animal advocates, for generations. Holly had been volunteering at a rescue for dogs, which is a lot of work. She also had a full-time job and was raising her daughter, Morgan, who was thirteen at that time. At some point, she decided to start her own rescue, which she still has currently. It's called RAD, Rescue A Dog.

I was telling Holly that Elix would be going to Florida in May because of work, and I was accompanying him. I then suggested we do a fundraiser for RAD, seeing I would be in Florida and it could be a Mediumship event. She loved the idea. We agreed we could do the fundraiser on one of the days we were there visiting.

With Holly's connections, we secured an amazing venue, the Ruth Eckerd Hall in Clearwater, Florida. I was so excited because this venue has big names who perform there. Days before Elix and I were heading down to Florida, Holly called me and asked if I would go on a local TV show called **Great Day Live** to promote the fundraiser. I would appear with another woman who was very involved with the rescue, and we would bring two of the dogs that were up for adoption. I answered yes before she even finished asking the question.

It was May 15, 2018, and I was driving by myself to the **Great Day Live** studio when I heard a siren and noticed a cop was right behind me, so I pulled over. He stopped me and told me I was driving over the speed limit. I had no idea whether I was or not because I was so nervous about appearing on the show. He gave me a ticket despite me telling him I was heading to the studio to promote a fundraiser.

When I got to the studio, I met the woman who was going on the show with me, and she was holding the leashes of both rescue dogs who were coming on the show with us. Another woman brought us into the green room as we waited for our segment to begin. One of the segments before us was for Sesame Street, and there were life-size Ernie and Burt puppets walking around. Of course, I asked them to take a picture with me as they were leaving.

A gentleman came into the green room and said they were ready for us. We walked in and were introduced to the hosts, Kendall Kirkham and Michael Clayton, former

NFL player. They were both incredibly nice. We were told where to sit and then the countdown happened: **five, four, three, two, one**, and we were live. The hosts talked about the fundraiser event for RAD, and the Mediumship piece. They asked me a couple of questions and then asked me, "Steven, will you stay for the next segment and read one of us?" I said yes!

After the commercial break, it was just the hosts and me. On the drive to the studio, I had a young male in spirit with me. During the commercial break before I was to read one of the hosts, I asked the young male whom he was connected to, and he told me Michael. The countdown happened again, and we were live. I told Michael there was a young male in spirit standing next to him, he felt like a brother or a cousin. Michael became emotional and immediately told me it was his cousin. Michael's grandmother also came through as I was doing the reading.

The hosts were so into the reading that they asked me to stay on after the show ended to continue it via Facebook Live. Of course, I said yes. The rest of the reading was fantastic, and Michael gave me a big hug when we were done. Kendall also enjoyed watching me read Michael; we all liked our time spent together.

That night was the fundraiser. There were about eighty people that attended the event. The room we were in was beautiful. There was also a silent auction to raise money for RAD. I was even more nervous than I was doing the show that morning; this was my biggest event yet. During my introductory speech to the audience, I remember a German Shepherd in spirit just kept running back and forth in front of me. So, I started with him and told the audience there is a German Shepard here. For the first thirty seconds to a minute, as I mentioned the dog, and no one was claiming it. Finally, a woman stood up and said that it was her husband's dog. The flow started at that point, and it ended up being such an amazing evening.

I remember going up to one table and reading this gentleman. His wife quickly told me he didn't want to come to this event and he was suspicious. I told him his grandfather in spirit was stepping forward and immediately I saw his expression change. There were many validations, but when I said, "Your grandfather wants to talk about the car," he broke down and cried. He had been working on this car with his grandfather and that time spent together meant the world to him. At the end of his reading, he stood up and gave me quite the hug.

It also was a great night financially for RAD. We were able to raise enough money to help many dogs in need. I was also very lucky. One of the guys that worked at the Ruth Eckerd Hall knew someone in the police department and was able to get my ticket dismissed. I was very appreciative of the kindness of this gentleman. Mostly, I was so thrilled that I was part of an effort to raise money for rescue dogs and I hoped to use my skills for more events like this in the future.

INSIGHT

One of the biggest lessons I have learned from spirit is that you must commit to always accepting and loving yourself. To understand and realize why you are here on earth, you must start with being genuine. The only way to be genuine is to accept exactly who you are and know how deserving you are. You can be aggressive and motivated to get what you want, but you will always be searching for that success and happiness if you don't understand that your first success was entering this world.

CHAPTER 16

THROUGH THE STATIC

I n 2017, I still had my probate business and did most of my legal work in Worcester Probate Court. My clients were hospitals and nursing facilities. I had just gotten into my car after finishing up a hearing in Worcester when my phone rang. I answered it, and a gentleman introduced himself as a radio host on WARA1320 AM radio in Attleboro. He told me that someone came up to him at an event he was attending and asked if he had ever heard of Steven the Medium. He said no and then looked me up. He was calling to ask if I would be interested in coming on his radio show as a guest. I said absolutely and we set up the date.

I was a nervous wreck when the day of the radio show arrived. The host had asked me in the previous conversation if I would be open to doing a couple of readings for people calling into the show. I had done readings using the phone before, but not readings on the phone, live, on the radio.

It was a wonderful experience; several people called in and the readings were fabulous. Subsequently, I visited his radio show as a guest several more times over the next few months.

It was early June 2018, and I was having dinner with Elix. I asked him what he thought about me having my own radio show on WARA1320 AM. He loved the idea. The next day, I emailed the station manager, Jim Jones, and told him my idea. He was very excited; he told me all new shows must be approved by the board and in two weeks, there was an open night for people to come into the studio and present what their radio show would be about.

Two weeks later, I showed up at the open call meeting. There were about five people there, sitting in a conference room, when I walked in. Jim walked into the conference room and led the meeting. Each of us had a chance to explain what our vision was for our potential radio show.

One guy introduced himself as Mark Clark, and said he had previous experience in radio and his show would be playing songs from the 1950's, 60's, 70's, and 80's. Thanks to my nerves I don't remember the rest of the subjects of the radio shows, and then before I knew it, it was my turn.

I explained that I was both an attorney and a Medium, and I wanted to do a radio show about spirit. The premise of my show would be people calling in and receiving a reading. I also mentioned that there was not a show like that on WARA currently. Jim smiled, but I had no idea if he thought it was a great idea or if I was crazy.

Within the next few days, I received an email that my show concept was approved, and it listed the necessary things I needed to get started. The first thing I needed to decide was the day and time of my show. I wanted it to be later in the day when people were on their way home from work or already home. I looked at the schedule and saw that Wednesdays at 5 p.m. were free. I thought the middle of the week sounded good, and I made my first decision on the show.

The second thing I needed was someone to produce my show. I thought that maybe I could produce it myself so I set up a date to meet with Jim about how it worked. He was going to train me on the software, the hardware, and everything I needed to know to be the producer.

About one hour into the training, the only thing I knew was I could not produce my own show and be the host at the same time. It was overwhelming to me. I told Jim the next day that it would be impossible for me to focus on doing a reading for someone and be aware of the time, breaks, answering the phones, etc. Then Jim got a great idea.

Jim had already trained Mark Clark on the production element for his show. His show was approved also, and he would be focusing on oldies music. He selected his show to be on Wednesdays from 3 p.m. to 5 p.m. Jim approached Mark and asked him if he would be willing to stay one hour longer, from 5 p.m. to 6 p.m., and produce my show. Mark has told me numerous times that what intrigued him was the subject of my show because he didn't have much experience with the whole spirit world. Mark agreed and I had my producer.

The third thing I needed to decide was, do I do this alone? That thought lasted in my head for about ten seconds because my next thought was to have Elix as my co-host. I asked Elix and at first, he was a little hesitant but quickly afterward, he said yes. I was so excited that Elix would be on this journey with me. I also knew Elix would say yes. He sincerely is the greatest guy in the world.

The fourth and last thing I needed to decide was what date to start my show. Elix and I talked about it and decided July 25, 2018 would be the first day on air. Mark was starting his show, Mark's Jukebox, one week before me on July 18th so I knew he would be available to produce my show on the twenty-fifth.

It seemed like the preparations I needed to complete for the radio show were done, until I realized that I didn't have a name for the show. It is not easy coming up with a title for any kind of show and I was having a hard time figuring something out. I then had an idea that I could do a contest via social media and have people write in a title they liked for the show. I thought it was a brilliant idea and the winner would get a free reading with me.

I put the advertisement together and posted it on social media. Immediately I started getting suggestions. I stated that the deadline to submit a potential title for the show was in a couple of days and once that deadline was met, I would review all the submissions and narrow it down to three.

Within a couple of days, I received over one hundred submissions with so many great titles. Elix and I reviewed all the titles, and I came up with my favorite three. I involved Elix with the selection, but I knew I had to choose the winning title myself. The day before the deadline, Elix and I met friends for dinner and we went to a restaurant in Providence, Rhode Island called Los Andes. The atmosphere and food were incredible.

Toward the end of dinner, our friend's son Ryan brought up my new radio show and the contest for the title of the show. Ryan's girlfriend, Julia, said "Is it too late to give you a possible title?" I said no, tell me. She said "What about Through the Static?" Immediately I got shivers through my body when I heard it. I thanked her and that title never left my head the entire ride home.

I had already selected the final three titles, but Through the Static became the top choice. I loved the title, but then I realized I also needed music to lead into the show.

That was also a difficult decision because I love music. Music has always been my muse and listening to it brings me to a higher frequency that is so close to spirit. I had my favorite songs, but how would I decide which one? A memory popped into my head.

Every year growing up, my family and extended family would go out for Thanksgiving dinner. For many years we would go to Venus de Milo in Swansea, Massachusetts for Thanksgiving. It was a banquet-style restaurant known for its soup.

But the real tradition was to go to LaSalette Shrine on Thanksgiving night. LaSalette Shrine has been a spiritual, social, and human service home to thousands of people from all walks of life for over sixty years. On their website it reads, "Our doors and grounds are open to all who need a place to quiet down, relax, and find the strength to begin again." LaSalette has been open for more than fifty years and is located in Attleboro, Massachusetts.

One fascinating thing about LaSalette is the Christmas lights. They have over 300,000 lights spread over ten acres of land. Thanksgiving night is the premiere of the Christmas lights, and the last night is New Year's Day. I have memories of going there every year since I was a little boy and I keep that tradition alive today.

I have a fond memory of one Thanksgiving when my cousin/sister Holly and I were in the backseat of my mom's car, leaving Venus de Milo and heading to Lasalette Shrine, and "Lotta Love" by Nicolette Larson came on the radio. Holly and I started singing it together and having so much fun. That created one of those memories that is never far away. That was all I needed. The song for my radio show was selected: "Lotta Love."

Elix and I were living in Norton, Massachusetts at the time, which is the next town over from Attleboro where the radio station is located. It took us about twenty minutes driving to get to the station. On July 25, 2018, we arrived at the station around 4:30 p.m. and peeked in the studio to see Mark doing his show. I was listening to Mark's show, and he was advertising this new show, "Through the Static" with Steven the Medium premiering right after his show. That was so cool to hear.

I was probably the most nervous I have ever been right before the show started. Elix being with me did help calm my nerves a little. Sitting in the studio, with headphones on and a microphone in front of you is surreal for someone's first time doing a radio show. When I listened to that first show, I could hear the nerves in my voice, but the show was terrific. I never thought I would have been capable of having my own radio show and after the show, I just sat and basked in the amazing accomplishment I had achieved.

INSIGHT

The majority of people are their own worst enemies. So many times, we put limits on ourselves without being aware that we are doing it. Sometimes the limiting beliefs come from our upbringing and what we learned from society. Oftentimes, we hear something that we think is beneficial but really it's just getting us "off the hook" so we don't have to do something that is unfamiliar or uncomfortable.

Here is a great exercise to resolve the limitations. I call it "stepping out of yourself." Find a place to sit and get into a comfortable position. Close your eyes and take about three or four deep breaths in (you know you are taking deep breaths if your stomach extends out as you are inhaling), hold the inhale for about five seconds, and then exhale. Always inhale through the nose and exhale through the mouth. Using your third eye, the area between your eyebrows, pretend there is a clone of yourself inside your current body. If your clone stepped out of your body and stood next to you, it would be like looking at twins standing next to each other. Using that visual, have your clone step outside of your body and walk behind you. By trying to stay with your clone in your third eye, get to a point that your clone is not only behind your body, but is looking at the back of your body. At that point, you are in the present and this is where all the magic happens. What is happening is you are separating yourself from your personality but not your soul. This is where you can start taking inventory of your life and challenging your beliefs and asking why in many areas of your life. This exercise will start chipping away at beliefs that have held you back in life, and start the process of letting go of those beliefs so you can fill that space with positive energy that aligns with your authentic self and will automatically put you in the flow of life.

CHAPTER 17

SPIRIT IS ON THE FAST TRACK

In Rhode Island, one of the news stations is WJAR. I mentioned this station and Frank Colletta in an earlier chapter, when my friends and I "explored" the station and a weather map. He did this online segment, in between newscasts called "Coffee Break." Frank also announced his retirement from the station, where he worked for almost forty-one years. I reached out to the producer, and he was very interested and excited to have me come on the segment as a guest.

On December 14, 2018, I drove to the WJAR station and met Frank. He is a very nice guy. I told him about who I was and then did a live reading for him. It was great and I loved getting to meet Frank before he retired just a few months after my guest appearance.

In December 2018, a friend of mine reached out to me about an event she was doing in February in Boston. It was going to be a three-day event at a hotel with several demonstrations with Mediums and speakers talking about evidence of life after death. She asked me if I wanted to be one of the Mediums. I said yes. Over the next few weeks, we exchanged emails with all the guests, and one of the things they decided was that if any of the Mediums wanted to do readings outside of their specified demonstrations, each Medium would charge the same amount. Ultimately, I didn't agree with the process and pulled out of the event.

I have never followed many rules throughout my life. Specifically when there is a group environment, I generally decide to do what I want to do and not follow the group. But in this instance, the process I disagreed with was something that should have never reached the level that I brought it to, and certainly should not have been something that would have made me pull out of the event.

My Paternal Grandmother, Rose

A couple of days later, I was in my bedroom and I heard, out loud, my paternal grandmother Rose say, "Get back into that event." That was the first and last time (so far) I have ever heard my grandmother Rose be so stern with me, and the first time I heard her objectively, meaning the same way I would hear Elix if he was in the bedroom talking to me. After hearing her speak, the only thing I could do was to somehow get back on that itinerary.

I told Elix what happened but also stated how in the world am I supposed to get back on the schedule. The last time I had spoken with my friend to tell her I was pulling out of the event was not a great conversation. But the more I thought about it, the more I knew I would rather deal with speaking to my friend about getting back on the schedule at the event as opposed to dealing with my grandmother Rose. She scared me!

I reached out to my friend, had a great conversation, and thankfully she put me back on the event schedule. I didn't think too much about why my grandmother Rose told me to get back in the event once I was back on the schedule; I was happy and stopped thinking about it. Little did I know how important it would be for me to be at that event.

On Friday, February 22, 2019, I showed up at the hotel. This is where all the guests would introduce themselves to the audience of people staying for the three-day event. There were about eight guest speakers/Mediums and I was the first to get up to the microphone and introduce myself to the audience. Unlike the rest of the guest speakers, after the introductions I left the hotel and wouldn't return until Sunday because that was my allotted time to do my demonstration. Most of the guests did not live in Massachusetts so they were also staying in the hotel.

On Sunday, February 24, 2019, Elix and I headed to the hotel because my demonstration was starting that afternoon. I had an hour and a half to do readings for the audience. The attendees totaled about one hundred people. I was told I needed to stand in front of the audience and not wander into the rows of where the audience was sitting because the event was being filmed and it would be too hard for the camera people to record me if I was moving all around the room.

I started my reading and tried my best to stay up front, but that didn't last too long. When I'm in spirit mode and having a three-way conversation with spirit and the person I am reading, it's hard to remember to stay in the front of the room, at least for me. Before I knew it, I was in the middle of the audience reading this woman and after each reading, I always hugged the person. They did film me and as far as I know, there were no issues with me wandering around the room and keeping me recorded.

When I was finished, many people came up to me to compliment me and to ask many questions. Some people, who were not read, were trying to get a mini-reading once the event was completed. I love meeting new people and either sharing my experience or listening to their stories. After I was told I was a Medium, but before much was happening in spirit, I scheduled a Medium to come to my house to do a group reading. There were only five of us in the group so it was very intimate. After the reading was done, I started talking to the Medium. I told her what a Medium had told me and the weird things that were going on around me. She responded casually with something about how the planets are aligned and how they will pass. I remember feeling so dismissed by her that I have said many times, I will do my best, for the rest of my life, to never make someone feel dismissed when they are talking to me about what's going on in their life connected to spirit.

As I was talking to some people, Elix came up to me, grabbed my arm and said sorry to the people I was talking to, and said he needed to steal me away for a bit. He brought me to a couple that was in the audience and wanted to be introduced to me. One of them was a former television producer who complimented me on my demonstration. She mentioned how specific and detailed my validations were, and how my style was very different from the rest of the Mediums presenting that weekend.

THE NEXT STATEMENT TOOK ME OFF GUARD. She said she has worked many years in television production and knows "star" quality, and I had it. Then she said, "You should have your own television show." I was trying to process what I was hearing, but coming off an almost two-hour event (I blew past my allotted time) and being exhausted, it wasn't easy.

On our ride home, I wasn't sure where that conversation would lead me, but at a minimum, to have a TV producer say I had star quality and should have my own TV show put me on cloud nine for the rest of the evening.

I kept in touch with the TV producer after the event and she introduced me to an individual who owned two magazines: **Hollywood Weekly** and **Hollywood Monthly**. For promotional purposes, I thought it would be a great idea to be part of one of those magazines. I had several conversations with him and ultimately I was featured on the cover of **Hollywood Monthly** in the September 2019 edition, with a fabulous article as well.

SPIRIT IS ON THE FAST TRACK

In November 2019, Elix and I went to Los Angeles, California. It was my first time in LA and I immediately loved it there. There was a group event set up at someone's home and I was going to do a Medium event for the group. I was told there would be a successful producer in the group, but I had no idea who it was when I walked into the room. The room was moderately sized but there were about twenty-five people, sitting on chairs, sitting on the floor, and standing around.

I did a reading for a gentleman, and interestingly enough, his dad in spirit came through and wanted me to do a private reading with him. Eventually, I figured out that he was the producer and we set up a date the next day for me to meet him and do a private reading. I went on and did readings for many people in the group and it was a wonderful experience.

I was so excited about doing a reading for a producer, but I was also very nervous. We scheduled to do the reading in the afternoon, so once I was showered, dressed, and ready to go, I told Elix I would go into the hotel's small living area and meditate, as I typically do to prepare for my readings.

I was in the middle of my meditation and Elix was in the shower when I heard a man's voice in my third mind. This meditation was one I used frequently so it took me by surprise when I heard his voice. I tuned in with him and he told me he was the producer's father and wanted to write his son a note. It took me a couple of seconds to process what I was hearing, then he told me to grab the hotel stationery and he would dictate to me what he wanted me to write.

I stopped my meditation and got up to find stationery. My mind was blown that this man was telling me to do this. Not only had I not ever done it, but it was also never on my mind as something I should try.

I sat back down on the couch, with pen and paper in my hand and lap, and waited for this man in spirit to start talking to me. I started with **Dear Son**. I didn't hear him actually say that, I just knew this is how the note should start. Then he started showing me images and quick movies, and saying names. I felt his emotions and without any kind of order, I just wrote down what I received. It lasted about one minute, and I wrote as much as I could in that short time frame.

When it was done, it looked like I had scribbled on a piece of paper. I started deciphering the words immediately, and tried to put a consistent flow on the paper so it made sense. When I was done, I signed it, "Dad," folded the paper, and put it in my pocket. I went back and forth, repeatedly, on whether I should give this note to the guy I was about to read in about one hour. I decided to surrender it to the universe and in the moment I was doing the reading, I would decide whether to give it to him or not.

When Elix and I got to the location where I would do the reading, the producer and I went into a separate area to get started. We both sat down across from each other, and I was giving him the introductory speech I always give before I start a reading. At that point, I pulled the note out of my pocket and said, "I have a note here that was dictated to me by your dad. Here it is (as I handed it to him) and it's up to you whether you want to read it now or hold on to it and read it in private." He quickly said he wanted to read it now, unfolded the note and started reading it. About ten seconds into reading it, he rose from the chair and said he needed a minute and walked away. I thought to myself, **Oh, what have I done?**

He came back within one minute and said the first couple of lines he read were like his father was still living and had just written the note minutes ago. He said he was stunned, but was ready for the reading to start. I started the reading and read him for about one hour. His dad started the reading but many of his loved ones in spirit came through to give him validation to make sure he knew it was really them.

He did read the entire note at the end of the reading, and reiterated how much the writing in the note resembled his father's writing.

THAT ONE NOTE WAS ABOUT TO MORPH INTO A BUSINESS. Two years later, I spoke to a guy who owned a social media company because I was interested in growing my social media network. He told me over the phone that he would email me a presentation about his company and how he could help me. The next day, I received his email.

I clicked on the link in the email, and it brought me to a screen with a video recording of him on one side of the screen and his company's presentation taking up the rest of the screen. He went through the three or four pages of his presentation by simultaneously highlighting parts of the document he was referencing, scrolling down the document, and explaining everything via the video recording. I loved the software and thought it was cool.

Out of curiosity, I emailed him and asked him what software he was using with this presentation, and he told me it was Loom. I thanked him for his presentation and knew I needed to do some more research before I committed to anything. A couple of weeks later, I revisited his email and was watching the presentation when I got hit with a bolt of lightning. I thought, I think I may have a terrific idea.

INSIGHT

One thing I have learned from spirit is you must work hard to find out what your reason for being here on earth is. Always starting with curiosity is the best way to begin your quest to find out what you are passionate about. To find your path, you must be willing to ask for and accept help from others. You can't do it alone. But you must be open to everyone who is willing to assist you, including your loved ones in spirit. We all have levels of loved ones, angels, guides, masters, and experts in spirit just waiting for you to bring them into your corral. On an ongoing basis, check in with them and ask them to be with you, to help you, or take the lead and do what's in your best interest. They will never let you down.

CHAPTER 18

A WHISPER IN A NOTE

As I was thinking about the Loom software, I was wondering if there was a way for me to utilize this software with notes I could send to people.

Sending notes was an idea I was forming for a new service I could provide; I would write notes for people with messages from their loved ones in spirit. The first thing I did was get a subscription to Loom. Once I obtained one, I started getting familiar with the software. My goal was to have a note on the screen, like the presentation was with the social network organization, and have a recording of myself explaining what was in the note. It took me a couple of days to figure it out and at some points I was frustrated because I was having issues making it work.

If I was to achieve my goal, I would need professional-looking stationery to write the notes on. I went to VistaPrint and selected a small note, five-and- a-half by four-and-a-half and started the design. When I got to the front of the card, I thought, **This must have a name.** I have always loved the word **whisper**, so I toggled back and forth with several names with whisper in them and ultimately came up with "Whisper in a Note."

In a few days, my Whisper in a Note and the envelopes were delivered, and I was ready for a trial run. I wrote a fictitious note using my new stationery and I scanned it into my computer. I then logged into the Loom software and started the preparation for doing a recording. With the Loom software open, I opened the Whisper in a Note I just had scanned into my computer. I pressed the record button and three-two-one-live!

As if this was being sent to a real client, I started with an introduction and then started reading what was in the note. I read every line and interpreted not only the words but also the emotions of what I would have felt from spirit if they were dictating the information to me.

Once it was done, I copied the link to the video presentation and pasted it into my email and sent it to myself. I then opened the email, clicked the link and it brought me right to the video presentation. I was so excited because it worked and looked perfect! The next step was to get it up on my website and start offering it as another service.

Since the Whisper in a Note has been offered on my website, it has been a big hit. A person can purchase one for themselves or purchase it as a gift. You can select whom you want the note from, i.e. father, mother, dog, etc., or not be selective and leave it up to spirit to decide who writes the note.

Several times I have taken notes with me when we are traveling, via planes or trains, and I have selected someone to receive a note. I did one when we were traveling to Puerto Rico. I tuned in to three of the flight attendants and asked spirit which one needed to hear from someone. I then focused on the chosen flight attendant and asked one of her loved ones in spirit to stand next to me and dictate a message to me. The flight attendant's dad came through and started chatting very quickly. I wrote everything down as fast as I could.

When I was done, I closed the note and put it in the envelope. I waited for the appropriate time to approach her and when I saw three of them chatting in the galley, I knew it was time for me to make my move.

We were in the second row, so it wasn't a long walk to the front of the plane. I introduced myself as Steven the Medium and explained one of the services I provide is to write a Whisper in a Note. I handed her the note and said this is from your dad. She looked at me, with eyes watering up, and said, "Oh my god, Steven, thank you. She also asked, "Can I read it now?" I answered, "Of course, it's your note." I then turned around and went back to my seat.

She disappeared behind the wall separating the galley from the seats so I couldn't see her. I assumed she was reading the note, but I wasn't sure. About three minutes went by and then she came around the corner, down the aisle, and stopped at our row. She had tears rolling down her face and said, "I don't know how this works, but that note was written by my father and I needed to hear from him so badly." She bent over and hugged me and said she would treasure the note forever. She also mentioned that she could not wait to tell her siblings and show them the note. Her response is the reason why I love what I do.

INSIGHT

When you love what you do, ideas, opportunities, and creativity are always a thought away. When you are following your passion, it's almost like things are handed to you without you asking for them. I have so much excitement for what I do in the spirit world that there is a part of my mind that is constantly looking for new ways to provide my service to people. I don't know where or how the idea came into my head when I looked at the Loom software, it just did, and it has enhanced my business on many levels.

CHAPTER 19

THE PANDEMIC

December 16, 2019 was the date of Elix's back surgery. Over the years, Elix had issues with his back, and they just got progressively worse. He was in a lot of pain, and it was interfering with everyday life and exercise. Even with pain in his back, he never stopped his weekly routine of exercising.

We go to New York City the second week in December every year, but this year was different due to Elix's back. He was in pain when he walked a certain distance, which isn't great for New York City, and the surgery was scheduled in mid-December. We reserved a hotel room in Boston because the surgery was being done in Boston at Massachusetts General Hospital;in case of any inclement weather, I wanted to ensure we would not have any issues getting back and forth to the hospital.

I was a nervous wreck as they were wheeling Elix away to prepare him for surgery, but I had already checked in with every spirit I could find to make sure they watched over him and everything would be okay.

After about five hours, the surgeon called me to tell me everything went great, and the surgery was a success. I started to cry because I was so relieved, and I asked when I could see him. A couple of hours later, I was able to see Elix and he was alert and looked great, especially after such a long surgery.

I stayed with him in the recovery area until about 10 p.m. and then headed back to the hotel. It was weird sleeping in a hotel without him, but knowing how well the surgery went allowed me to get a great night's sleep.

The next morning, I went back to the hospital and was in awe when I got to the floor Elix was on and saw him walking in the hallway with a nurse. I was really shocked, but I was more excited to see him walking already.

The nurses working on the recovery floor were outstanding. One nurse that was assigned to Elix for the day would be in and out of his cubicle. Every time she came in, we would chat with her about everything. When the shifts were changing, a new nurse walked in and introduced herself to us. After a couple of minutes, she looked at me and said, "Are you Steven the Medium?" Before I could respond, Elix said, "Yes, he is!" She told me a friend of hers had a reading with me and she follows me on social media. It turned a great day into a greater day. As we were chatting, I heard a guy in spirit say, "Tell my daughter her dad is here." I hesitated for a moment, but I trusted spirit and did what he told me to do.

I told the nurse a father figure was standing next to her, and she got so excited. She told us her dad had died about three years ago and she thinks about him every day. I went on and started doing a full-blown reading, with her grandparents coming through and even her dog. She was already emotional but when I mentioned the big dog, like a retriever or lab, she got even more emotional telling us about her lab that the family owned and how much she loved her.

Another nurse walked by the cubicle, peeked in, and saw her co-worker standing next to Elix's bed and crying. She came in to see if everything was okay. The nurse I was reading told her why she was crying and the nurse that stopped in stayed and then I did a mini-reading on her. Before you know it, I think I read almost all the nurses on the shift leaving and the shift coming on. It was fantastic!

The nurses also loved Elix. They delayed Elix's transfer to the main hospital floor as long as they could so they could keep us with them. Elix and I were both sad when we had to leave the recovery floor. Those nurses were incredible.

The next day, Elix was transferred to the regular hospital floor. It was a double room, and no one was in it when we arrived. Elix was allocated to the first bed as you walked into the room. The nurse that greeted us in the new room was very nice. I knew Elix would want the second bed, the one next to the window. I needed to be crafty, so I decided to tell her who I was and give her a mini-reading. Listen, spirit doesn't have an issue with that. They only care that they get to tell their loved ones on earth they are still here!

I finished the reading, she loved it and then I made my move. I asked her if there was any way Elix could take the window bed. She said they were very strict on assignments there, but she would see what she could do. She left the room and minutes later came back and told Elix to bring his stuff to the next bed. Elix and I smiled and thanked her many times. She may have moved Elix without the reading, but I killed two birds with one stone. I got to do what I love, and I got Elix the bed with a window view.

My mom had been in a nursing home for a couple of years. Before we moved her out of her house and to the facility, we had nurses and aids coming to the house to help. My mom never went to see a doctor. My entire life I never saw her seek medical assistance. I tried for years to get her to see a doctor just for a check-up and she always refused. In 2010, I noticed she was repeating things and asking the same question a couple of times. I finally convinced her to see a doctor, and after some tests and an MRI, we were told she had had several mini-strokes. I was shocked because I never saw any physical change in her. The doctor told us that the strokes caused the beginning of vascular dementia and that was the reason why she was repeating.

She was still working as a crossing guard at eighty years old. With no exaggeration, she looked like she was no more than sixty years old. That same year that we found out about the strokes, she retired and as the years went on, the disease progressed. It then got to a point where she needed more care than I could give her. The biggest issue that was occurring was her falling; if it happened after the help left for the night, she wouldn't be able to get off the floor. If she couldn't reach her cell phone to call me, she would have to stay on the floor all night. Once it became a safety issue, I knew something had to change.

It was a spring day, April 13, the day we were moving my mom into the nursing home. Because Elix had been in the healthcare industry for many years and had established great relationships, he was able to get my mom into a wonderful facility.

I told Elix I couldn't bring her because it would be too hard for me. Elix and my best friend, Paul, went to my mom's house to pick her up and bring her to the facility. My other best friend, Susan, came to my house to support me. As it was happening, I didn't stop crying for a moment. My mother and I were best friends, and even though I knew it was the best thing for her, it was still tearing me apart.

Elix called me when he was leaving the facility and told me my mom was talking to everyone there, and when he said he was leaving, she kissed him and said bye. Hearing that helped me a lot, and she acclimated to the facility quickly.

In January 2020, my mom started declining. Her appetite slowed down and she hadn't been vocal for about one year. Covid was being talked about on the news, but I don't think anyone had any idea what we were in for at that point. Life was still the same despite hearing about this new pandemic. The week prior to February 12, 2020, the nurses were preparing me for my mom's crossing as she was eating very little or not eating at all. On February 11, I went to the nursing home early with the plan to stay the entire day. Elix came by in the morning but had to do some things for work and said he would come back a little later.

It was about 6 p.m. and I was sitting next to my mom in her bed and Elix was next to me. I could see and feel all our family that was in spirit all around the room with my dad on the other side of the bed next to my mom. The one thing that is not easy for a lot of Mediums is to read themselves. Trying to connect with my loved ones in spirit that were in the room was not easy. I knew they were there but the communication, I think, is a little more complicated.

With Elix behind me, I was holding my mom's hand and said to her "It's okay to let go. I know everyone is here waiting for you to join them. Ma, I love you." She looked right at me and with pure clarity said, "I love you too." I couldn't stop the tears from falling and I whipped my head around to Elix and asked him if he heard her. He smiled and said of course he did, as plain as day. My mom hadn't been vocal for such a long time, so this was a miracle and a way for my mom to say goodbye.

I left her room and the facility around 10 p.m. and went home to sleep. I knew I would wake up early, shower, and head back to the facility. On February 12, I was dressed, had car keys in hand, kissed Elix goodbye, and headed downstairs to the garage to head out when Elix's phone rang. What I didn't know was that Elix had told the director of the facility, when Claire dies, please call me and not Steven.

Elix motioned me to stop, and I knew right at that moment. He hung up the phone and just stared at me. I asked him, did my mom die, and he said yes. There are some things you never forget, and this is one of them. With car keys in hand, I dropped to the kitchen floor and wept. After losing my dad at eight years old, I never thought this day would come. All I ever had was her, my mom.

My mom was very close to her dad. After she got married, she moved to South Carolina because that was where my dad was stationed in the Navy. Her dad died when she was in South Carolina, and she always talked about how she regretted not being with him when he died. I used to say to myself that would never happen with me and my mom, I would be there when she crossed.

I wasn't with her when she took her last breath. The funny thing is when I'm doing readings, I have heard spirit validate that they purposely passed when their loved ones were not with them because it would be too hard to leave with them by their side. My grandfather, Fred, passed that way and then my mom did the same thing to me.

My nephew Tristan and his then-girlfriend (they are married now) were driving up from New York City to see my mom the day she passed away. Elix called Tristan to let him know the news. Tristan recently told me that at that moment, he debated whether to turn around and go back to New York City as he still had about three hours to drive to the nursing home. He decided to keep driving to Massachusetts and I am so happy he did.

Elix called Paul, who owns a funeral home in Rhode Island, and he and one of his staff drove to the nursing home. It was so comforting to know my best friend would be taking my mom to the funeral home.

When we left the nursing home, Tristan told me he was going to drive back to New York City that day. Despite my offer for them to stay with us overnight, he still decided to drive home but I offered to at least bring them someplace to eat some food before they headed back to New York City. They agreed.

Elix, Tristan, Maria, and I went to this restaurant called the Chateau in Norton, the town we lived in at that time. The restaurant is abutted by a beautiful lake and the table we sat at overlooked the lake.

MY MOTHER WAS ALWAYS OBSESSED WITH THE SKY. She loved looking at it and if there was a beautiful sunset, she would boast about it. We were done eating and we were just chatting and waiting for the check. I looked out of the window and the western part of the sky was gorgeous. I didn't think too much about it and pulled my cell phone out and took a couple of pictures of the sky. I reminded everyone how my mom loved the sky and pointed to how gorgeous it looked.

We left the restaurant and Tristan and Maria started their drive back to New York City. Later that night, Elix and I were lying in bed watching TV when I thought about the picture of the sky I took at the restaurant. I opened it up on my phone and something made me zoom into the picture. I honestly thought I was seeing things. In the mix of the clouds and the sun trying to beam through those clouds, were letters that spelled out *C L A I*; the *R* and *E* were not as clear, but you could see them. My mom's name, Claire! I jumped off the bed. Elix didn't know what was going on and I told him to look at this picture and to tell me if he saw something specific.

I handed him the phone and he stared at the picture on the phone for a couple of seconds. His head looked up at me and said I see Claire spelled out. Not only did my mom use the sky because she knew I knew how much she loved it, but she also somehow spelled out her name in the sky. This happened about five hours after she crossed over. I have saved that picture in many places to ensure I will always have it and be able to look at it.

My Mom, Claire

One month after my mom passed away, I had to cancel all my in-person Mediumship events because of Covid. The world was closing quicker than I could ever have imagined. There is no doubt in my mind that my mom intentionally chose February 12, 2020 to cross over, one month prior to everything closing. She knew the effect it would have had on me if I couldn't have access to her and see her in the nursing home because of Covid restrictions. I have friends that had to deal with not seeing their parents for months due to Covid, and that's not something my mother would have let happen to me.

INSIGHT

Anybody living in 2020 had never experienced a pandemic like Covid. These were unchartered waters, and we were forced to take one day at a time. One thing that spirit has taught me is as soon as you trust and believe that your life is meant for you, you can handle anything that comes your way. There will be times that you do not like your life and what is happening in it, but if you remind yourself that your life sees the bigger picture and knows exactly what needs to happen for you to keep growing, it will be so much easier.

CHAPTER 20

THE LADY OF THE DUNES DOCUMENTARY

I t was February 18, 2021, and I received an email from Frank Durant. He said he was a Massachusetts-based filmmaker and was producing a documentary in April on the Lady of the Dunes. He also stated for the documentary, he was looking to work with a Medium that can give their expertise on finding the truth about her murder. If I am interested, please let him know.

On the same day, I received an email from a producer of a Miami-based television series that was looking to have a Medium appear on one of the episodes. We emailed each other back and forth for a couple of weeks, but ultimately the show decided not to use a Medium so that was off the table. The producer never told me which show it was for, but I think I figured it out from the little information I received from her. She was so nice and thoughtful!

I responded to Frank on the same day and said I was interested, so we set up a phone call so he could tell me more about the documentary. Even though he told me the murder occurred on Cape Cod, despite living here, I had never heard about the Lady of the Dunes story. Prior to talking to Frank, I Googled the story and read all about it.

The story is about a woman who was found murdered in the dunes at Race Point Beach, Provincetown, on July 26, 1974. As of February 2021, the case was the oldest unsolved murder in Massachusetts. The woman had no identification, and the murderer was also never identified.

I had never used my Mediumship for a murder investigation, but this documentary sounded so interesting. After our conversation, Frank offered for me to be part of the documentary and I gladly agreed. Frank told me he reached out to thirty Mediums across the country, and every one of the Mediums was interested in being part of the documentary. I was thrilled beyond belief that I was going to be in my first documentary!

Frank told me filming for me would be on April 9, 2021, and he would give me more details in the upcoming weeks.

About two weeks later, Frank called me to give me an update on the documentary. He mentioned the three other Mediums and I stopped him and said, "There are other Mediums in this documentary?" He said yes, but it was the first time I had heard about this. In that conversation, I told Frank I did not want to interact with any of the Mediums and didn't need to know who they were. This had nothing to do with the other Mediums, it came from a place of making sure this documentary represented me in a positive way. I told Frank, if you are looking for someone to be part of a circle of Mediums, chanting and looking crazy, you have the wrong guy.

Filming "The Lady of the Dunes" Documentary

I took a chance saying that to Frank because I could have been removed from the documentary, but this experience was new to me and I was being protective of my reputation. Frank told me that wasn't a problem and I quickly realized he was a genuine and amazing filmmaker.

Frank gave me the schedule of filming and I was to appear on April 9 at St Peter's Cemetery in Provincetown at 10:30 a.m, and later that same day at the previous home of the 1974 Police Chief Jimmy Meads Sr., at 6 p.m. The cemetery is where the Lady of the Dunes was buried with her gravestone reading: **Unidentified Female Body Found, Race Point Dunes July 26, 1974.**

I decided to drive to Race Point Beach on April 7, 2021, two days before I was supposed to film my part in the documentary. I walked onto the beach and found a spot in the sand and sat down. I brought a notebook and pen with me and the first thing I did was meditate. The meditation was to connect with the Lady of the Dunes; I asked her to step forward and tell me what happened the day she died and anything else she thought would be helpful. I had been checking in with her over the previous days to build a connection with her and hopefully gain her trust. On the drive to Race Point Beach, I knew she was riding with me in the car and we had already established a great relationship.

At the end of my meditation, the Lady of the Dunes stood in front of me and held her hands out for me to take hold of them. It was incredible because her hands had been cut off when she was murdered, and I then realized she was letting me know she had her hands back. She stood next to me and started giving me information. As fast I could, I scribbled down everything she told me. Once I got home, I would decipher the notes and put them in my formal note card. When she was finished, I thanked her and told her I would do my best to make her proud.

Frank emailed me and told me he made reservations for us for the night of April 9, at a hotel in Provincetown called Eight Dyer Hotel. I was also excited because this was the first hotel I was staying at that was paid for by the director/producer. Elix and I arrived at the cemetery around 10:20 a.m., and we were greeted by Frank and his camera people who were already holding their cameras. There were three of them and they were directed by Frank. Elix and I walked up to Frank and he asked if we wanted any of the coffee or donuts that were sitting behind him. I was so nervous, there was no way I could drink or eat anything at that point. I told Frank about the note I wrote, dictated by the Lady of the Dunes, and I handed it to him. He asked if he could read it and I said of course. He was fascinated with the note and thanked me for doing it and giving it to him.

Elix and I were introduced to his assistants and then we heard, "We have two minutes." Frank said we were ready to start filming. He then directed me to walk over to her grave and start talking. "Connect with her and whatever you feel like bringing up is fine," he told me. I was shocked because I thought I would have more direction. I heard, "Take one," and I had no choice but to start walking towards her grave. I reached her grave and squatted down and placed my hand on her gravestone. I asked her to let me know what she wanted me to say, and she started talking.

She started talking about her life and reiterated some things that I had written in the note. I also remember removing the mask I had on, due to Covid, when I was bending down to touch her gravestone. I loved that this documentary would capture the pandemic influence on all of us as we were filming it.

Elix and Frank were behind the scenes, listening to me and watching the camera people film me. Elix told me after the shoot that Frank looked at him during my shoot and said, "Either Steven has connections with a lot of people or he is really talking to the Lady of the Dunes because what he is saying, no one knows about." It was so amazing to hear that.

After the shoot was done, we had the rest of the day before I was scheduled to do the second shoot. Elix and I love Provincetown so we walked down the main strip, Commercial Street, and stopped at a place to have breakfast. We did a little shopping afterward and just enjoyed walking around in this magical location.

Jimmy Meads Sr., as mentioned above, was the Police Chief in July, 1974, when the Lady of the Dunes' body was found. Jimmy had two sons, Jimmy Jr. and Michael, who still lived in the area. Jimmy Sr. passed away in 2011.

The house where Jimmy Meads Sr. and his family grew up was now owned by two women. Across from the house is the Eight Dyer Hotel. That hotel is owned by a married couple, Steve and Brandon. Frank negotiated with the owners of the house so that we could film in their house. The two sons, Jimmy Jr. and Michael, hadn't been in that house since the family sold it years ago. Frank thought it would be nice to be in the environment where Jimmy Sr. lived for many years and raised his family.

One of the requirements from the current owners was that Steve and Brandon were onsite the entire time we were filming so they could keep an eye on the house and make sure things went smoothly. I believe the ladies were in Florida at the time; they split their time between Provincetown and Florida.

We arrived at the house around 5:45 p.m. and were introduced to Steve and Brandon. We were also staying at their hotel across the street. These two were the nicest guys, and Elix and I are now very good friends with both of them. Frank came out of the house and invited us in. I met both sons, Jimmy Jr. and Michael, and Michael's daughter Emily. There were three camera people recording, and the reading was done in the living room at a big dining room table.

Jimmy Jr. and Michael sat at one end of the table and I sat at the other end. The reading was well over one hour with their dad coming through and giving wonderful validations. At one point, Jimmy Sr. referenced his granddaughter Emily who was in the living room sitting and watching with others. The validations he gave her were so emotional that she was in tears. She loved her grandfather, and the feeling was mutual.

The Meads brothers were also the nicest guys and were happy to be part of the reading. I was honored to be the one Medium out of four that got to not only meet the brothers, but do a reading with them. Most of the reading does not appear in the documentary. Because so much of the reading was very personal and emotional for the family, out of respect, Frank only put two small meaningful segments in the documentary.

I was so relieved once we were done. I knew the reading went really well and my part of the filming was completed. Elix and I went to dinner to celebrate and stayed over that night in P-town.

Frank's purpose in doing this documentary was to shine a light back on this unsolved murder that happened almost fifty years ago. His hope was to help identify the Lady of the Dunes and her murderer. Frank and I had many conversations over the next few months, and I always told him that the Lady of the Dunes said this documentary will be big and help things move forward on many levels.

At the beginning of March 2022, Frank told me that the documentary was completed, and he had two premieres set up. On April 1, a screening would be held at the Cape Cinema in Dennis, Massachusetts at 12:30 p.m., which is a couple of towns over from Provincetown, and the other on April 2 at Provincetown Theater at 7 p.m.

I was so excited that a documentary I was in was going to be screened in a theater. At that point, I had not seen the documentary so I would be seeing it for the first time with a lot of other people.

One day I was sitting at my desk in my office when I got an email from Frank telling me the screening in the Provincetown Theater was sold out. I just stared at that email, took it all in, and I wanted to tell Elix immediately. I could not wait to be sitting in those theaters and watching the documentary.

Elix's cousins, Eva and her daughter Mariana, came from Puerto Rico to be at the premiere. We are very close to them, and I was so in awe that they were flying in from Puerto Rico just to see the documentary. The four of us drove together on April 1 and headed to the Cape Cinema. This theater was large, and I was so impressed by how many people were there. I was even more surprised when I saw some people whom I have done readings for sitting in the theater to see the documentary. I felt so humbled and honored.

Frank introduced the documentary, and it started playing. About halfway into the documentary, the subject of Mediums starts and that's when I come on the screen. I am the first of the four Mediums to appear, and it was surreal to see myself, on this big screen, in a theater. When I appeared, Elix grabbed and squeezed my hand and we both got to experience the moment together. When it was over, the feedback was incredibly positive. People that noticed I was in the documentary came up to talk to me and some asked for pictures of me with them. I loved how people also wanted Elix in their pictures.

April 2 was a Saturday. My two best friends, Paul and Susan, had planned to come to our house and drive with us to see the premiere in P-town.

Cousins Eva and Mariana were also coming again with us, which I loved. We got to Provincetown earlier so we could all go to dinner before the premiere. We had a terrific dinner together, and then walked over to the theater. As we were walking into the theater, the people in front of us were told that the show was sold out and they turned around and walked by us to leave. That still gives me chills.

I was stunned again to see people who follow me on social media and whom I had read to be sitting in the audience, and it was so great to chat with them before the show started. Frank introduced the movie again, but this time I met him on stage and handed him a thank you gift for doing this documentary. This was Elix's idea, and I am so happy Elix thought of that.

Both sons, Jimmy Jr. and Michael, and their families were at this premiere. This showing was special because it was in the same town where the Lady of the Dunes was found. After the show, the feedback was again very positive. It was amazing to see the wonderful reaction from everyone who just watched the documentary.

Over the next couple of months, the documentary was screened at a couple more theaters. In July 2022, it was screened at Waters Edge Cinema in Provincetown. Frank had a family emergency so he couldn't attend this screening. I was honored to be the one to introduce the documentary in his place, and afterward I did a Q&A for the audience. I also did the same at another theater.

Two days later, on April 4, we were leaving for vacation to Palm Springs and Los Angeles, so these couple of days were the best! The trip to California was for pleasure, but also for business. Elix and I were creating a series called "STELIX," a combination of our two names, which would be mini-episodes of our lives. We were introduced to a fabulous editor whom we hired to edit the footage we filmed to create mini-episodes.

We completed three episodes and premiered them on my YouTube channel. The episodes are playful and fun, and the locations go from Puerto Rico to New York City.

Both of us had so much fun recording these episodes and are always in awe of how the editor turned them into mini- episodes.

It was the morning of October 31, 2022, and I was again in my office doing work. I received a notification that there was breaking news and that there would be a press conference happening soon about an unsolved murder that happened many years ago in Provincetown. I got chills when I read the notification and I knew immediately that it was in reference to the Lady of the Dunes.

I called Frank but got his voicemail and told him to call me. I then texted him the same thing. He called back about ten minutes later, and I asked him if he heard the news. He said no, so I told him what I had just read. He started digging through social media as we were on the phone and found the headlines about the news conference. He told me he would let me know if he heard anything and we hung up.

Ironically, I was doing my first Mediumship event in Provincetown that night at the Waters Edge Cinema. I was going to do readings for the audience and then the original Hocus Pocus, a Halloween movie the owner and manager of the theater let me pick, would be shown in the theater.

I knew the Lady of the Dunes coordinated this press conference on the same day my event was happening in Provincetown as a thank you for everything I did for her with the documentary.

The press conference was later in the afternoon, and it was held in Boston with the governor of Massachusetts, local police, and the FBI. After almost fifty years, the Lady of the Dunes was identified. Her name was Ruth Marie Terry. When I completed my note with the Lady of the Dunes a year and a half ago, I asked her how to end the note. Should I write a name or initials? She told me to put the initials **RAD** and I did. It blew my mind that her first name was Ruth and the first letter in the initials was **R**.

The next few days more information about the murder trickled in. The Lady of the Dunes was married at the time of her murder to a man named Guy Muldavin. He was a suspect in the murder of his previous wife and her daughter. He was questioned after the Lady of the Dunes murder but was never held accountable. There were other things that were publicized about Guy, and he quickly became the number one person of interest in the murder of his wife, the Lady of the Dunes.

When I was communicating with the Lady of the Dunes and gathering information for the note, I asked her, "Who killed you?" She responded that his name began with a **J** or **G** and he had lost a son, which changed his personality. I don't see letters when spirit is talking to me, I just hear them. Lady of the Dunes responded with a **jah** or *gah* sound, so that is why I put either a *J* or *G* because they sound similar and are interchangeable with certain names.

Guy, with a *G*, did have a son with a previous woman but she had enough of him and took off with their son. He didn't have a relationship with his son when they left and that affected him severely.

The validations from the news conference that connected to what the Lady of the Dunes had me write in the note were unbelievable.

On August 28, 2023, it was announced that this case was closed with the conclusion that the Lady of the Dunes' husband, Guy Muldavin, killed her. Just like on October 31, 2022, Elix and I were in Provincetown when this was announced. Another wonderful thank you from the Lady of the Dunes. There are also several years missing from the Lady of the Dunes' life and there is speculation that she may have been married before. Will that explain the *A* and *D* from her initials *RAD*? Even with the case now closed, you never know what may be validated in the future.

INSIGHT

As a Medium, I had never worked on a criminal or unsolved case before. Because I was getting good at what I did with people and their loved ones in spirit, I almost boxed myself in with this as my specialty, and started thinking it's all I could do. Periodically, you must stop and ask yourself, "Is there something I am missing in my life? Have I put a tight corral around myself without realizing I can open that corral and reach a broader scope?" Many of us develop tunnel vision when we get comfortable with our lives.

If you are comfortable, you are not learning. Get comfortable being uncomfortable (I picked that saying up from Elix) because that is where the magic is happening.

CHAPTER 21

LIVING IN THE PRESENT

I believe one of the biggest gifts spirit has given me is to remember to live in the moment. That is not something I have done for most of my life and not something I understood before. Most of us do not live in the moment. Sometimes it's not easy to live in the moment due to our lifestyles. Life moves so fast due to technology, and that forces us to move that quick. Most of us are not aware of our surroundings. How many times do you drive to work and either don't remember passing a certain part of the road you drove by, or maybe notice something on your way home and say, "How did I drive by that and not notice it earlier?"

It's very easy to know when you are in the present because you will be happy with an incredibly peaceful feeling that washes over you. If you love the beach, imagine sitting, with nobody in sight, on the beach and listening to the waves crashing in front of you. You feel the warm breeze passing by you and the occasional sound of a seagull flying by. Your feet are nestled into the sand, your eyes are closed, and the sun is warming your entire body. Your body sinks into the chair, and you are thinking of nothing else except where you are at that moment. That is living in the present.

However, you do not need a beautiful atmosphere like the one mentioned above to be able to be in the present. Elix and I went to New York City for a weekend this past January and we stopped in this store in the mall. Elix was trying something on in the dressing room and I was waiting for him. I focused my attention on the present by looking around, being aware of my body, my presence, and that Elix was right behind the dressing room door. Nothing else mattered except that moment, and everything around me felt energetically heightened. I then had a wave of gratitude flow right through me and I loved that I was with Elix, in New York City, having this experience with him. It was an amazing feeling.

I try to remember to be conscious of being in the present every day. I have noticed that the more you do it, the more it happens and the easier it gets.

If Elix is having a difficult day and saying negative things, I will always remind him that the longer he stays in that frequency, the more time he is wasting and preventing himself from moving forward. He does the same thing for me. It's not always easy to be receptive to hearing this when you are in a certain mood, but the words stick with you and help to get you out of that frequency more quickly.

Something else I have learned from spirit is the importance and connection of energy, intention, and feelings. Understanding that we are all made up of energy i.e. humans, trees, dogs, frogs, flowers, etc., enables us to get what we want sooner. If I have a goal, I never say I want this, or I know I will get this, or I am hoping I will get that. All of those statements tell the universe you want it and keep you in a position of always wanting it and not having or experiencing it.

In 2020, Elix and I decided to sell the house we had lived in for fifteen years and move to another place. We both always loved Cape Cod but over the years we had always been concerned that we couldn't afford a house on the Cape.

Elix said he would like a house near the ocean and the woods for privacy. I agreed but I also told him that it would not be easy because if you are near the ocean, generally you do not have a lot of woods around and the houses are not far from each other.

In the summer of 2020, we started speaking about our intention to live in Cape Cod, connecting our energy to a house in Cape Cod, and feeling what it would feel like to live in a house we owned in Cape Cod that was close to the ocean and had woods around it.

We put our house on the market in August 2020, and it sold in two weeks. I found a house for sale on Cape Cod that wasn't listed on the main real estate websites, and I wasn't exactly sure how I found it. I emailed our real estate agent, and she had no knowledge of the house or address. She did research, found it, and set up an appointment to see the house.

When we went to see it, we were in shock. This house was four minutes from the ocean, had a pond in the backyard, and abutted twenty-plus acres of conservation land. We immediately fell in love with it, made an offer, and have been living there since November 2020. Intention, energy, and feeling were a big part of us getting to our dream house.

We are currently working on several big projects that we are very excited about. The people we are working with are genuine, authentic people that have the best intentions. Spirit continues to bring us opportunities that keep moving us forward. I can't wait to see what I encounter as I continue on my journey. Spirit has taught me to look back at all my accomplishments, breathe in what's happening right now, and feel what lies ahead.

My dad's suicide changed every particle in me. It wiped out most of my internal structure and replaced it with a foreign structure, one that I didn't know how to communicate with. It created a new trajectory for me to follow with no GPS and new obstacles at every curve. But it also created this box, wrapped in gorgeous gold paper with a big blue bow. I always knew it existed but had no idea how to access it or unwrap it. Recently, both eight- year-old boys walked up to each other, opened their arms, embraced, and at that moment, merged into each other leaving only one eight-year-old- boy. Now standing alone and powerful, the present appeared, and he was able to unwrap it and reach into the box to pull out the gift. The gift of being a Medium.

www.ingramcontent.com/pod-product-compliance
Lightning Source LLC
Chambersburg PA
CBHW030304130626
46549CB00002B/689